ACCIDENTAL
MADNESS

ACCIDENTAL
MADNESS

At The Intersection of
Extreme Creativity and Entrepreneurship

a memoir

David Wiener

DWV

ACCIDENTAL MADNESS
At the Intersection of Extreme Creativity and Entrepreneurship
a memoir

David Wiener

ISBN: 979-8-218-41201-2
Photo Credits: Most of the photos are by David Wiener.
Others are used by permission.

Book design by David Wiener
Cover photograph by Peter Brush 1984
Published by David Wiener Ventures

Printed in the United States of America
PO Box 982470 Park City, Utah 84098 USA
info@DWV.com
Visit www.DWV.com

A master in the art of living draws no sharp distinction between his work and his play; his labor and his leisure; his mind and his body; his education and his recreation. He hardly knows which is which. He simply pursues his vision of excellence through whatever he is doing, and leaves others to determine whether he is working or playing. To himself, he always appears to be doing both.

—Francois Auguste Rene Chateaubriand

For Kate.

Every entrepreneur needs a loving partner who can endure the roller coaster ride, bring a laugh, and not give up when the going gets tough.

Raising three wild sons while on the roller coaster made it that much more exciting.

Here's to Weston, Hans and Enzo!

CONTENTS

THIS IS NOT EASY

I'VE HAD TWO TO THREE HOURS OF SLEEP each night for more days than I can count, and now I am about to launch one of America's greatest athletes on a world speed record attempt. His vehicle, riding an inch off the ground, is a long missile-like three-wheeler of my creation. It has never run in full race-ready trim, and there is no real protection, safety margin, or idea of how it will go. A PBS television crew has been chronicling my every move, following me and my team around like remoras. A journalist even lived with us in the week leading up to the event, scrutinizing me, like the crush of spectators and fans who are all here on the promise that we are the team to watch—the team that's going to make history. Everything I have is riding on three wheels. Every ounce of my being is strung out to the point that trying to herd my team while trying not to make a single mistake could be the end of me. The three-wheeled contraption I envisioned, designed, engineered, and built—it has to work. It has to. Not just for my ego, my sanity, and the joy of the lookers-on, but for the safety and well-being of my rider. Yep, just another day in Wiener World.

I spent the past seven months dreaming up and executing this mad exercise in hopes of finding fame and fortune while making history. Somehow I raised funds and recruited two Olympic champions as "engines" for my streamlined, human-powered vehicles. I snuck into shops to use their milling machines, talked a long list of vendors into sponsorships and discounts, skipped holidays and vacations, and focused every bit of my mind and muscle on achieving something amazing. And now it's showtime. No room for excuses, no do-overs, and no room to half-ass it. The prior year's speed-record winner, a team of engineers from General Dynamics—the defense contractor giant and builder of nuclear-powered subs, jet aircraft, and a slew of other highly advanced goodies—had set an impossibly high bar. But no turning back now—it's *go time*. Crowds are cramming in. Cameras are rolling. Earth has stopped spinning. And to think, I'm doing all this just to graduate college.

That was just one of many in a long series of madcap ideas and ventures that I've been involved in. At the time, words like *entrepreneur, marketing,* and *return on investment* were unknown to me, and it would be years before anyone could benefit from the convenience of things like CAD, the internet, Google, Excel, PowerPoint, Photoshop, and so much more. In other words, I jumped into *my* world when I was twenty, with little to no understanding of what business—and being an entrepreneur—was about.

But it was never about being an entrepreneur. It still isn't. It's always been about creating, inventing, designing, and realizing a dream—over and over and over again. Through it all, I've become, or always was, an entrepreneur.

These days, people think being an entrepreneur is glamorous. That it's cool. That it's easy. That it's like being a rock star in the business world. But that's all hype.

Being an entrepreneur is dangerous. It's taxing. It's scary. In the darkest moments, it will make you question everything. It seduces you into thinking that extreme times justify extreme measures. Theft. Suicide. Crazy stuff. Yet the thrill of creating something new, unique, and innovative—something most people would think impossible—is what draws me back in again and again. I have an addiction. I must raise the bar. You may think I'm joking, but I'm dead serious.

I started making and selling "stuff" at eleven. By sixteen, I was a professional sports photographer with an agent and assignments shooting America's Cup yacht racing, the Indy 500, US Open tennis, and more. I wasn't a fan of school. It moved too slowly and mostly in directions that I had no use for. But I was really driven. This cocktail of creativity and drive led me to engineering, aerodynamics, and art in college, my idea of a perfect combination for a future dedicated to creating custom cars and more. At twenty-three, I was recruited out of college by Paul MacCready, the most famous engineer in America at the time. At twenty-four, I started my own company. Within a year I had furniture in showrooms in New York, Dallas, San Francisco, and Paris. At twenty-five, I was manufacturing recumbent bikes and had built a series of custom Porsche 911s for clients. At thirty-one, I was reengineering ice cream mixing systems as a consultant to Ben & Jerry's and assisting Nike with their shoe beds. Later, I'd be asked to design a ground-effects aircraft for Flarecraft Corporation and a novel fly fishing clothing brand for Columbia. The list just grew from there.

I have started a number of companies, some of which have been successfully selling my products for many years. I've sold products around the world, had endless media coverage, met interesting people, and realized long dreams of working with Ferrari, Porsche, and other global brands. I've had great successes and a few failures. I've employed a couple hundred people, worked in many countries, and set up production on several continents. I've raised money, lost money, made money, and always, always used money as fuel for the next project. And regardless of where the financial needle pointed at the end of each one, whatever we created was always at the sharp end of the spear in terms of innovation, design and performance. That, and that alone, was always my goal. Best of all, I am still doing this and do not plan to slow down.

As I write this, I have design, technology, and fashion projects in the works, while also creating artwork for public spaces and corporate lobbies. I also advise clients on *their* projects, manufacture high-end products, write articles for automotive journals, and dream about the long list of things I still want to achieve. But with all of this comes an endless amount of stress, heartache, and worse. It's not all champagne and big bank accounts. In fact, many less creative entrepreneurs are often far more financially successful as they can focus better on the business at hand—but we'll get to that later.

Being an overly creative entrepreneur takes a toll. The stress, the financial burdens, and the impact on relationships add up. On many sleepless nights, I've often called into question why I ever wanted to be an entrepreneur. Wait, did I ever really say, "I want to be an entrepreneur?" No. What actually happened was the evolution of my need to create self-imposed challenges, a symptom of wanting to impress my father. Over time, I realized the absurdity of that age-old conundrum, but I retained a permanent drive to excel—to push limits and do it my way. And what better way than to work for myself? I was compelled to create products, brands, and businesses. I just wanted to make that next thing, launch it into the world, and get a reaction. Decades later, I still do.

Sometimes those reactions were great, and sometimes, well, the word *brutal* may be sugarcoating it, but like an addict who needs that fix, I returned again and again.

When I use words like *drug* and *addiction* as allegories for my career choice, it's not harsh or hyperbole. Creating something from your mind and bringing it to life provides a rush few other experiences come close to. There is no high like watching your idea being manufactured and shipped to people who plunked down money to buy it, or seeing your creations featured in international media like *Fortune, Forbes,* and *Newsweek.* Sure, we all feel good about ourselves when our mothers say, "That's a great idea." But when total strangers say it's a great idea and vote with their wallets, all the blood, sweat, tears, and dollars that went into the dream are vindicated.

Of course, there is always a price. I had to embrace business, and like any serious businessperson, I've gone through that risk-and-reward evaluation baloney. The problem is, when you're all in on creating, somehow the ability to logically compare the two evaporates. To that end, I've done things like mortgaging my house, hoping the gamble would pay off before I was eaten alive by my bet—or my wife! I've drained my bank account to zero. I've sold off prized possessions, maxed out my credit cards, and begged and borrowed to breathe life into my dreams—dreams that produced ungodly amounts of stress.

Although universities pride themselves on their entrepreneurship programs, there's a wide chasm between the classroom and the street. I never took any entrepreneurship classes, but I can assure you that nothing can prepare you for that moment when you know you are responsible for employees, when you know they are placing their trust in your dream and expecting a paycheck to feed their families. That's a reality check! The weight of having to meet payroll for other families sometimes felt heavier than the responsibility to my own family. Then I got to know and found I liked those people, making it even tougher. The thought of not being able to pay them caused me to think about driving my car off a cliff—really—on more than a few occasions. Cheating people out of their earned livelihood was not something I could live with, and no three-credit college course will ever teach an engineering, art, or entrepreneurship student about this. Thankfully, I never did turn the wheel, instead refocusing my energies and making payroll. Every time.

Today, people use *entrepreneur* as a catchall to describe anyone who builds a business, from the Bransons, Ellisons, and Musks to the hot dog vendor on a street corner. But what about the creative person who just wants to bring an idea to the market? No one ever talks about that. They just use a new catchall: *maker*. People throw the *entrepreneur* word around like it somehow applies to anything related to making money. They also tend to focus on the glamour of those entrepreneurs who've made it really big, the ones whose names are household words. I'd be lying if I didn't say I wish I was one of them, but I know the realities. Real success stories at that level are rare, and I also know that success is much more than just fame or a headline paycheck. While we hear about those few who seemingly became billionaires overnight, it's the story before the monster money moments that create success.

If billionaire is your measure, you'd better choose a different line of work. Reality is weighted against you; you don't even have a one percent chance. On the other hand, success can be found at all points along the path: paying off a mortgage early, employing dozens of people, finding purpose in one's work, or in my case, creating the best-in-class at whatever I'm doing. That's my addiction. Fact is, even on vacation, I can never stop working, which constantly frustrates my wife. It's persevering through the highs and the lows that pays off for the driven entrepreneur. It's the journey, the adventure, and the experiences that occur during all the peaks and valleys of the emotional roller coaster that color the success story.

My roller coaster ride has been both thrilling and exhausting but never boring. Whether in the worlds of Formula One and Ferrari or high fashion, cyber-encryption, and international artwork, my fuel of choice has been stress and pushing myself to the limit. That has meant figuring out how to make something, getting it to market, and ensuring it's seen as innovative, exciting, and desirable.

Everything I've ever created has been at the intersection of performance and style. There was always a clear path for me: dream the excitement, then work on it. I custom-tuned my career to focus on things that were exciting to me, even when people around me were telling me, "That's impossible!"

My real dilemma: I never plan to retire, but I do hope to one day figure out how to answer the dreaded question, "So, what do you do?" I never know what to say. Which portion of my activities I should focus on? I can't tell the whole story. I can't do an ego rant. And mostly, I don't want to let them down. I want to be unique in their memory, but I don't want to be absurd. I just always want to move on to whatever the next question may be.

There was a moment a few years ago when, over some bourbon, I asked Blaine Parker, a Park City friend and marketing pro, how I should approach this question. He wrote an elevator pitch trying to capture who I am and what my company, David Wiener Ventures, is. It was embarrassing. It was accurate, but it was too much. I tried to distill it down. My career in four words: *I create extraordinary products.* I can't say this. Next question please ...

This is not a how-to book. If you want a *Ten Things You Need to Become a Successful Entrepreneur*, you can get that in a thousand different flavors. My stories are meant to illuminate what unbridled drive, creativity, and entrepreneurship are really about, good and bad, sane and insane. They are told with raw honesty because, while these are my stories, my hope is that many will resonate with you, get you to think, inspire, energize, and provide a few laughs as you pursue your own dream.

This isn't the easy I-have-a-great-idea-so-I'm-going-to-be-rich activity most assume it is. But it sure is thrilling—every day! It really is. I often wake up in the middle of the night, excited to get to work. Sometimes that's mixed with fear, but I'm always eager to try something, anything, to achieve the next goal. It's a sickness, one that I will never cure.

Forty years in, the list of products, apparel, vehicles, technologies, and brands I've created, not to mention the clients and partners I've had along the way, have provided me with countless adventures and stories. Let's start at the beginning.

CHAPTER 1

I'M AN ENTREPRENEUR?

SOME OF THE MOST UNLIKELY people have become successful entrepreneurs, while many of those voted Mostly Likely to Succeed fell flat on their faces. Among those who succeed, the consistent demonstrated behaviors seem to be creative thinking, optimism, drive, passion, and risk-taking. Whether someone was born that way or became that way—well, honestly, I don't care.

The reality is I can only speak for myself and about the adventures I've had. After many years on this path, I found there was a name for what I'd been doing: *entrepreneur*. That's how most people would see it. But on closer analysis, I was all about a hypercreative drive. As a kid, I didn't know I was being entrepreneurial. I didn't even plan most of it. I didn't know I was ever going to go into business or manufacture things. I just wanted to create stuff. But I'm getting ahead of myself. Let's start with a little introduction . . .

I grew up in Westport, Connecticut, with an artist father and a doting European mother. As you might imagine, creativity reigned supreme with my father, and he believed that only artists, people who created art for art's sake, were worthy of respect. Anything commercial missed the bar for him. Lucky for me, he had basic hand tools and showed me how to use them, including a band saw and a belt sander. He also had an unbridled need to share his endless opinions on "bad" design, "ugly" buildings, and worst of all, his disdain of money, and the people who focused on making it. With that in mind, I decided I wanted to make a lot of money so I could *do* things. Buy things. I had to balance that with my growing need to meet his standards. All of this was self-imposed—a psychiatrist's dream.

Figuring I had to hustle, I began my creative escapades early. Unlike the lemonade aficionados of my neighborhood, I started inventing and making *things* to sell. According to my mother, I was that kid who was never without tools. As a toddler, I'd run around, clutching my plastic hammer, saw, and screwdrivers. I had to hunt for parts, whether around the house, in my dad's studio, or at junkyards, to create my "inventory." My creative, driven personality blossomed during my childhood. Back then it wasn't business, it was simply a way of making some money and trying to have fun doing it. I made enamel jewelry, peace-sign medallions, hippie bead necklaces, and other unusual items to sell around the neighborhood. This cemented my desire to work with tools, make stuff, and create the things I "needed," like a go-kart, a hydroplane, and speaker cabinets for my electric guitar—you know, simple stuff. I did this by cajoling my way into free lumber, scrap parts, shop time, and advice, all at a very young age.

Along the way, I learned that sales are a measuring tool. If a kid's lemonade didn't sell, the downside was a bit of wasted time; Mom sucked up the cost of the sugar and lemons. I, on the other hand, had more skin in the game. If my items didn't sell, it wasn't only a waste of "manufacturing" and sales time but also a challenge to my ideas and perhaps my young self-worth.

Making money was important, but it was never the sole desire or driving force. Sometimes my raw enthusiasm for whatever I was doing drove me, and sometimes it was the result of my father's constant ragging. He never missed a chance to bemoan anyone earning a normal living, from Wall Street stockbrokers to even graphic artists (that one really surprised me). At the time, I just soaked it up and believed he was the oracle. Boy, did I have a lot to learn.

We all know that our parents' words from our childhood can have a serious afterglow in adulthood. My father's ability to be hypercritical (and often hypocritical) was more about him opining than it was about actually helping or teaching. He offered his opinions, whether they were wanted or not, throughout my youth and well into my professional life. More often than not, they were negative, insulting, and uninformed—but the hits kept on coming. As an example, it never mattered to him that I was truly committed, from a very young age, to a life of racing cars.

I knew the direction of my life by age six. While most five-year-olds were fascinated with Silly Putty and building blocks, I discovered pictures in my mother's French magazines of Le Mans and Formula One racing cars. That was the launch point. I ate, slept, and dreamed car racing. I even convinced my *Oma* (grandmother) to use her sewing talents to make me my very own racing suit: classic '60s light-blue fabric, one-piece design, and a Ferrari patch on the chest. Absolutely perfect. Forget that I was six and would've worn a light-blue burlap sack—I was thrilled. Little could I imagine then how my affinity for Ferrari would come full circle nearly five decades later with a phenomenal business partnership. Or that I would ultimately design fashion for motorsports and beyond.

Here's a classic example of my dad in action. At seventeen, I had worked like mad to afford my first car, and my budget meant I was going to be buying something in less-than-stellar condition. Worse than substellar, I had to rebuild the whole thing, from the engine to bodywork and paint to interior upholstery. After finishing it enough to be drivable, I got the idea to start making it even better. I decided to paint racing stripes on the front hood that matched my racing hero Peter Gregg's Porsche race car. No sooner had I finished the paintwork than my dad came outside, saw what I had done, and responded with, "Boy, you really fucked that up!" He wasn't talking about the quality of the paintwork. He was commenting on the design of it all. Nice. Years later, he'd make a similarly soul-crushing comment during an interview for the PBS documentary about me, *Human Power*.

My father's parenting approach had two main byproducts. On the positive side, his method, though hurtful, was and is a constant force pushing me. Somehow I converted what might have been a spirit-draining force into a motivator of sorts. That hypercriticism causes me to continuously question the quality of everything I produce. I am unable to take the easy way out or cut corners. It also serves as my mental devil's advocate, examining issues from multiple sides. In the end, I am constantly trying to impress my biggest critic: me.

On the negative side, there is a danger of being your own worst critic. I've often looked at the products or brands I've created without taking the time to acknowledge that there might be something good there. It's that voice that says, "So what?" Don't get me wrong, humility is a good thing, but too much of it isn't because you never take time out to appreciate your own accomplishments. It took me decades to realize this.

Thankfully, my mother was my father's polar opposite, so I had the yin and yang of parenting. Her support and confidence in me were constants, making her, in many ways, my earliest promoter and cheerleader. My mother's was the voice that often said, "Sure. Why not. Go ahead. Of course, you can." She remained calm through many of my harebrained adventures, smiling reassuringly while she thought, *So, my son's a little crazy.*

To my mom, her kids were everything. She had an unparalleled appreciation for life, all the way to ninety-two. She brought this to everyone around her: family, friends, and even the customers she served. She partnered with Martha Stewart at the Common Market, a boutique food store in Westport, Connecticut, before the age of boutique food stores (and before Martha was *Martha*). Later, she worked at such elegant boutiques as Hermes, Bottega Venetta, Henri Bendel, and others. My mother was modest, but she was truly an arbiter of style. Maybe this is why she was always positive and proud as she absorbed, supported, or promoted my early kid creations. I could always count on her to chauffeur me to the lumberyard and to not tell my dad about the charges on the hardware store account. I managed to make her mad a few times, but we both survived things like me mixing fiberglass resin in the basement, thereby filling the house with toxic fumes, or nearly wrecking her Mercedes when my rusty first car fell off the jack stands, stopping just shy of her pristine sedan. I don't think she really understood most of the projects and things I created, but that never stopped her from being supportive.

Being a designer and entrepreneur for more than four decades allows me certain freedoms and the ability to discuss experiences and realities, both good and bad. Confidence and enthusiasm for my work allow me to be honest, knowing I have, and can, overcome the ugliest bits. I am not going to pretend that I had a grand plan from a young age or that I even considered or understood how my childhood would impact me. Perhaps my early experiences were completely random events. More likely, those events built upon each other. In hindsight, I see three common themes: creativity, passion, and energy. But don't for a moment believe that I knew what I was doing.

Wanting to create for a living, I "designed" my career so I could dream all day long. I love creating, solving problems, brainstorming, and at times, competing to have the best idea or solution to a problem. I also love manufacturing, the making of things. When I was in fifth grade, we built a home in Westport, and the carpenters all drove station wagons completely filled with homebuilt toolboxes—veritable rolling hardware stores. I thought, *What could be a better life than having your tools and gear with you at all times?*

As a young adult, I often looked to experienced (i.e., older) people for guidance and advice. My college advisor, Herb Bernstein, a renowned quantum physicist and advisor to US presidents, would constantly push me to avoid manufacturing and focus on the "thinking" part of product creation, saving the labor part for others. Herb would tell me, "You don't really need to worry about all the fine engineering details, David, because you'll have people working for you who can figure all that stuff out. You're the creativity guy." Later, as I started my first company, Tom Feeley, a sage advisor and veteran of the Levi's company, would use the phrase, "No M"—no manufacturing. He figured I had so many ideas, why waste time and resources on the drudgery of production, sales, and marketing? Well, that didn't happen.

I didn't listen to my early mentors who told me not to manufacture because I simply love to see things being made. I am so committed and passionate that it's hard to hand off a design and hope another group will realize the product or garment or vehicle or graphic with the same attention to detail that I would bring to a program. The branding of the US Ski Team is a perfect example of one such graphic "product." For twenty years, a revolving door of outside designers constantly messed with the logos and image details my company created for the ski team, leading to improper uses of their logos and poor design by their people, sponsors, suppliers, and even counterfeiters. A brand must be controlled, especially one as global as the US Ski Team.

I keep a list of things I want to design and create, and I'll never get it all done. This tells me (and my family) that I will never retire. Why would I? I have too many things I want to do. Bottom line, I feel guilty almost every day because I am constantly telling myself I am not getting enough done and not getting these new product concepts to market fast enough. It's a curse I love.

The payoff is always the feeling of total elation when people see and react to my work. It's probably vain and full of ego-tripping, but who cares? When people get wowed by something I've created, it's a huge deal. The interesting thing is that I recently realized I do this stuff for me, not for them. I want to be wowed! My work, and that of David Wiener Ventures, are typically high-visibility items for high-profile customers and global brands like Ferrari, and I only want to work on exciting things. After all, if you have to work, why not do it on things that excite you?

WONDERAMA. This may have been the unexpected start. Mixing early creativity and risk-taking behavior began early. I was about seven years old when my brother and I got to be in the audience for Sonny

Fox's hit Saturday TV kids' show, *Wonderama*. This was mind-blowing for a little kid. On the appointed weekend, we were dressed up and taken to the TV studio in Manhattan and dropped off with a few hundred other kids. We were shown to our seats among a sea of chairs on the studio floor. Once we settled in, a production assistant wheeled out a hot dog cart—a thrill for a certified hot dog junkie like me. As they fed the overenergized mass, a chubby old guy went through the crowd. He was Joke Guy. On every show, Sonny Fox had a segment called "Joke Time," during which kids would tell Sonny a joke or riddle, try to stump him, and win a prize. Joke Guy's job was to audition kids who wanted to tell a joke, letting them test their joke out on him. If your joke was worthy, Joke Guy would give you a little card with the word *joke* printed on it, and you were instructed to gather around Sonny when he announced the "Joke Time" segment.

This was a real chance at stardom. A cameo with a TV star—all in front of your friends out in TV land. When Joke Guy asked us all, "Who has a joke for Sonny?" I enthusiastically raised my hand. On my turn, I took a break from my hot dog and gave it my all, butchering some silly elephant joke that was popular at the time. It bombed. I bombed. I was devastated. My big chance had come and gone. Clearly, Joke Guy had no sense of humor.

I sat and stewed, wondering how things could've gone so terribly wrong. Then the lightbulb went off, shining a light on my then-dormant risk-taking side. My brilliant, terrible idea: I'd make my own joke card. How hard could it be? I turned to various kids seated around me and awkwardly asked if anyone had a pencil and paper. It's hard to believe any young kid in that audience would be so equipped, but I got lucky. A kid nearby had a pen, but he grilled me on why I needed it. I could tell he was going to be tough to crack, so I quickly invented the ridiculous story that, although I had already received a joke card from Joke Guy, my little sister at home would surely be thrilled if I brought her one, and I needed paper and pencil so I could create a copy for her. What was I thinking?

Anyway, the kid finally gave in and lent me his pen. I quickly wrote "JOKE" in my best big block letters on a small scrap of paper I'd torn to resemble the real business-card-sized joke cards. I was all set. Eureka! I stuffed the ersatz card into my jacket pocket and waited.

This may truly have been the first entrepreneurial act of my life. I set a goal. I planned. I took sizable risks. I put myself out there. I realized the challenge. Most of all, I wanted the payday—the prize. In this case, it was an actual prize. If I was staggeringly lucky, I'd win an amazing prize, maybe even the plastic electric guitar on display!

The show got underway with games like Simon Says, cartoons, and other kiddy entertainment. It was torture. Waiting with my nerves on fire, I lost interest in most of the amazing Wonderama excitement. I was just trying to survive until "Joke Time."

Finally, they announced "Joke Time." I was exhilarated and petrified all at the same time. They asked the joke card holders to come to center stage and line up. I left my chair and shuffled along with about eight other kids, all of them bigger than me. I waited my turn to stand next to Sonny Fox and tell my joke. Cue the nerves.

No doubt I was causing a prime-time freak-out in the control booth. They had to know I was an interloper, yet what could they do? When it was my turn, I stammered through my joke, whatever it was, and naturally, Sonny Fox—Mr. Amazing to us kids—knew the punchline. Damn. I got pushed along with a crummy consolation prize: Flash Gordon swim fins—for your hands. Ugh.

The walk back to my seat was excruciating. I'd failed miserably—but I'd done it! I went for it before *going for it* was even a phrase in my head. A *start* was born.

We moved to New York City from Connecticut for two years so my dad could be closer to the art scene. I was eight, my brother ten, so my parents signed us up for PeeWee football with Shelly's All Stars, the best part of which was getting introduced to Nathan's hot dogs at Coney Island after Saturday practice. No, the real best thing, given that I was far more excited about car racing than football, was that I figured I could take the facemask off my football helmet and convert it into a racing helmet. Just don't let Dad know!

I snuck a knife from the kitchen, hid in the closet, and sawed and hacked away at that plastic-mask nightmare for days. I made a mess of the thing but finally got it off and had the beginnings of my first race helmet. With tape and model paints, I was sure I could create something I would be proud to wear. I can't remember my parents' reaction to all this, but I'm sure it wasn't good. Never mind, I was on my way. Any time the movie *Grand Prix* played on TV, I'd sit on the edge of my parents' bed, wearing my helmet while driving away with a plywood disk for a steering wheel, absorbed in John Frankenheimer's fantastic reproduction of the 1966 Formula One World Championship. Heaven! Of course, I did this when they weren't around.

In the 1960s, like most boys, I was also captivated by James Bond and *The Man from U.N.C.L.E.* I figured Illya Kuryakin had to be the coolest secret agent on the planet, and the modular gun he used was a study in tech (though I didn't know that word at the time). I was able to satisfy my thirst for cool hardware and managed to procure the toy version of the U.N.C.L.E. gun and its many amazing modular attachments. I still can't imagine how I talked my way into that treasure.

I think the U.N.C.L.E. weapon rubbed off on me in more ways than one. Aside from my lifelong involvement with guns and hunting, I've since created many products and clothing pieces based on modularity, where a main device could be enhanced through a variety of attachments and add-on features. What a great way to make a single product so much more effective and exciting. As examples of this, I created a line of World Cup ski racing wear for CB Sports that included modular race wear and coaches' coats, allowing skiers and coaches to add additional padding and protection from slalom gates and long hours on their feet or knees. Another was my patented push-powered lawnmower that could turn not just a mower blade but also a broom head, tennis court sweeper, leaf blower unit, and more.

By second grade, my love of music also filled my daydreams. I was a fully committed Beatles freak—so committed that two years earlier, I tried to give myself a Beatle haircut using kitchen scissors, which did *not* impress my parents! In second grade, we had a woodshop class, and I exhibited my energized spirit yet again. I told my teacher I wanted to make a bass guitar just like Paul McCartney's. While the other kids were making wood-and-macaroni sculptures, I was cutting a three-foot-long bass guitar out of ten-inch pine. With assorted screws for knobs, sheet metal cut to resemble the pickguard, nailed-on old guitar strings, brown paint, and a makeshift strap, I was in heaven playing air guitar with my "official" Beatles bass.

My new guitar looked cool, and even as a nine-year-old, I understood that such accessories could be a chick magnet, and that my guitar was. I proved this during our gym class free times when I recruited my friends Michael Delacorte, Peter Frankfurt, and Matthew Gaines to pretend we were the Beatles. I somehow convinced two of the cutest girls in our class, Cathy and Deidre, to pretend they were frenzied fans in hot pursuit. With me as Paul (thanks to my Beatles bass), we four boys would race around the gym floor, gabbing in absurd English accents, calling out to each other using our Beatles names, and letting the girls keep up. Some might say we were crazy . . . yeah, yeah, yeah. But this would later lead me to crazier experiments in rock and roll.

About the same time I was making my bass guitar, I was increasingly tempted by the treasures on display at the hobby shop I passed any time I walked home from school. The standout was the Eldon science lab kit, a mass of test tubes, rubber stoppers, tweezers, and a cool set of shelves to display it all. I saved up money made from scavenging and returning soda bottles to the corner grocery store. As my coin pile grew, I could feel it. That chemistry set was going to be mine—all mine! I just had to figure out how to get it home without being discovered, as I was certain my parents wouldn't have been too excited to have a mad scientist in their apartment. Add to this that my dad was very controlling about what I spent money on, a form of kid torture that continued even into high school. When I finally bought that kit, I realized being a mad scientist was impossible without a Bunsen burner—only the coolest item in any serious laboratory. Well, I had no idea how to get one, so I determined I could simply make one to begin my diabolical experiments.

The crazy thing about my behavior at the time was that it resembled entrepreneurial behaviors I've exhibited daily in my career. While most kids would have seen that chemistry set and maybe thought it cool, this was where their thoughts ended. The thought of *not* owning it never factored into my way of thinking. I knew my parents would never buy it for me, but it was a foregone conclusion in my mind that come hell or high water, the kit was mine. As it turns out, demonstrations of such optimism are an essential ingredient for entrepreneurship, though again I will say I had no clue about this for many years to come. I was also realistic enough, even at a tender age, to understand my parents' boundaries (not that they stopped me). This sort of reality check is an important element in the entrepreneur's psyche, confronting issues and creating a work-around or knowing when to stop the madness. (That last part I hadn't quite developed).

Finally, the day arrived. I bought the chemistry set and snuck it home. Next, I concocted a plan to create my very own Bunsen burner. All I needed was some kind of glass bottle, a wick, and some fuel. Simple. I knew I couldn't (or shouldn't) steal from the school's science supplies, so instead I found a random bottle, made a top with aluminum foil, and formed tissue into a wick. I kept this masterpiece of manufacturing hidden, knowing all too well what the consequences might be if it was discovered by my parents. I was giddy.

The hardest part of all this wasn't hiding the chemistry set and Bunsen burner in the room I shared with my brother. No, the trickiest part would be the fuel. *What does a Bunsen burner run on?* I wondered. I perused the flammables section of the hardware store down the block from my school. The colorful metal cans just screamed danger and excitement. On just the right day, when I had more coins saved up, I walked into the hardware store, swapped three dollars of hard cash for a can of something (Alcohol? Paint thinner? Nitro?), and made for home as quickly as I could. You really have to wonder about those days when a third grader could buy a can of flammable fun. "No, thank you, sir. Just this. I don't need anything else." Did they just not care, or did they think this eight-year-old had everything under control?

The timing was perfect. That Friday night, my parents had dinner guests over, so we were holed up in our room. While my brother and Gorman Cook, the kid from the second floor, watched TV, read comics, or whatever, I filled my Bunsen burner, getting ready to go into full mad scientist mode. My laboratory was my wood desk that had a nice covering of clear contact paper, that 60s-era self-adhesive clear film used to protect "important" surfaces. Everything looked just right for ignition. I snuck the metal can out of my secret drawer and proceeded to pour part of the contents into the burner's bottle—and easily as much onto my desk. I installed the makeshift top and wick and lit it as fast as my little fingers could get a match out of the pack.

If you ever want to truly test your parents' resolve, calmly walk into the middle of a dinner party and announce that your desk is up in flames. Then turn and run!

The ensuing inferno was nothing short of amazing. It scared the crap out of me, got the attention of my brother and Gorman, and ended my career as the next Dr. Frankenstein, all within the span of just a few minutes. Funny, I never saw that green Eldon science lab again. It just vanished. What didn't vanish was my desk. Charred and coated in melted, sticky plastic, it was mine. All mine!

Did I mention I also built a series of large wooden guillotines during that period? Oh, my poor parents . . .

One of the few highlights of those two years in Manhattan was going to concerts at the Fillmore East, a sort of educational babysitting dished out by my parents, with my guitar teacher as chaperone. At such a young age, I had no clue how important the Fillmore East was (or would become) in the world of rock and roll, but one thing was certain: I was transfixed by the amazing bands—three or four per night—and the psychedelic light show that was the standard backdrop for each concert. All I wanted to do was become a rock guitarist and live in that world (when I wasn't dreaming of racing Formula One cars around Monaco).

Many decades later, I would reconnect with the creator of those light shows. The Joshua Light Show, as every concert poster and program highlighted, was the brainchild of a then-teenage kid, Joshua White. He figured out a way to mix colored oils and water and create trippy, visual tie-dye projected onto a massive screen. I never forgot those shows or the hypnotic trance that the Joshua Light Show put everyone in, so around 2014, when I was launching a music sound-enhancement app with our Aphex studio recording technology, I sought out Joshua and ended up meeting with him several times to discuss adding his visual art to our Audio Xciter® app. Events like this always surprise me. The idea that a memory from so many years earlier could inspire a business opportunity or creative pursuit seems so hard to believe, but I relish those moments and celebrate the fact that some of my memory isn't shot. After all, there are days when I test myself by trying to remember what I had for dinner the night before.

It wasn't long before we were back, living in Westport again, where that music bug bit me some more. The year 1968 was a great time to love rock; it was the heyday of Jimi Hendrix, Cream, the Doors, Johnny Winter, and so many more greats who would go on to become legends. For me, the bonus round was that a Staples High School student somehow got both Cream and the Doors to play concerts at our high school auditorium (look it up—it's true). Forget that I was ten years old—I was going! And once again, the music, the guitars, the two bass drums, the clothing, the hair, and maybe most of all, the monster Marshall amp stacks sent me into a dream world where all I wanted to do was live that rock-and-roll fantasy. And live it I tried. In fact, I started smoking cigarettes with the cool kids on our street at every possible chance. How much more rock and roll could I be? Thankfully, by fourth grade, I dialed it back as my Kings Highways school buds had not yet made that jump.

While my guitar playing and time performing in bands didn't amount to anything close to a dream, the impact of those moments, the style, the performances, and the imagery left a permanent scar on my impressionable brain. The music creativity die had been cast, and it would surface many years later in the form of professional music and audio products, graphics, and more.

With our family now back in Westport, my dad got himself a studio in Greenwich Village. It was the late '60s, so there was no shortage of cool stuff to do when we'd spend weekends there. The biggest benefit to me, though, was that his building on La Guardia Place had leased its street-level retail space to what would quickly become the most respected guitar store in New York: Dan Armstrong Guitars.

As a guitar rocker in training, I had devoured every Fender catalog I could get mailed to me, so when Dan Armstrong opened up his small store, it was like having a guitar art gallery as a home base. Lucky me, I got to be that little kid who just hung around watching and absorbing the top talent that wandered in. I'd head downstairs from my dad's studio and spend every moment I could fantasizing and trying to interpret all the stuff Dan, his guys, and his customers were talking about.

Dan was cool. He knew my dad from the building, and he knew I was a guitar fiend. One day, when it was finally time for me to upgrade my electric guitar, Dan found me a well-worn Fender Jaguar and, later, a used Fender Pro Reverb amp. I was so over the moon I could see Mars. I can still smell the aroma of that classic Fender hard-shell case. Some months later, I even got to jam with John Cale, one of the founders of the Velvet Underground, who had a loft in the building. It was a dream, especially considering I was so young I could barely lift that Fender amp by myself.

My guitar playing came in handy when I ran for president of the Kings Highway Elementary student council. In the close race with incumbent Jan Moshe, my campaign featured a live cover of Cream's "Sunshine of Your Love," reworded by my campaign managers, Tim Woodruff and Mark Fenelon, which no doubt was better than my big speech. I was not the favorite of our school principal, having been forced to eat too many lunches in her office as punishment for various infractions, but I got back at her in the best way possible. I ran for class president and won. Funny thing is, I don't think my parents ever realized I was president of our school! Did it matter?

Between fourth and sixth grade, my desire shifted to creating things I could sell. My dad was a modern stained-glass artist and taught me how to cut glass and solder lead, so I started with stained-glass peace medallions on chains and other stuff. But I set my sights higher.

I got hooked by the ads in comic books promoting the amazing prizes you could get based on the number of boxes of greeting cards or packets of flower seeds you could sell. I signed up. I sold like mad to all the nice ladies in our neighborhood. With my bike, a catalog, and a sales kit, I was in business. I sold and sold and was thrilled by the cash and the prizes, a Cox gas-powered dune buggy being the biggie for me. So cool!

At the same time, I discovered photography and dove deep into taking pictures. Just like the cool mechanics of cars, cameras intrigued me, so I made attachments for my ersatz Instamatic, an Agfa camera that I knew would be so much cooler if I glued on a pro-looking sunshade, an eyepiece made from a suction cup, and a neck strap like all the Nikon pro guys used. At twelve years old, I'd already embraced the idea that even if I didn't have all the right equipment, I had to look the part. The same held true when I decided to do a custom paint job on my electric guitar a la Eric Clapton in the Cream years—yet another project I did in secret, knowing all too well that my dad would freak out.

While the early years got my motor started, adolescence got my juices fully flowing, and the adventures only got wilder and riskier as I stretched the bounds of parental control and personal safety to an even more dangerous degree.

CHAPTER 2

EARLY DAZE

AS A YOUNG KID, I EXUBERANTLY RAN on a nonstop treadmill of projects and ideas. I say *exuberantly* because I was eager to try everything and anything. My energy was matched by my total disdain for anyone or anything that got in my way. I was just excited to achieve and achieve some more, all in the name of making cool stuff to outfit my daily life. From amateurish experiments in making big speaker cabinets for my guitar to building hydroplanes and other kid-cool stuff, my days were full, and school was merely a distraction and an inconvenience. Here's a taste of what I thought made sense as I jumped headfirst into an assortment of creative adventures.

In sixth grade, infected by the car-racing bug, I announced to my parents and friends that I was going to build a go-kart. I'd checked out every go-kart book in the kids' section of the Westport Library, so I was armed and dangerous. I had my construction plans, and I saved every penny from my adventures in making and selling stuff.

Lacking proper funds, I was reduced from building a normal steel-framed kart to making one out of two-by-fours and plywood. Unlike my shop teacher from third grade, my seventh-grade shop teacher pumped the brakes, telling me, "You can't build a go-kart out of wood." And there it was: the most magical of fuels. My new lifeblood. He'd thrown down the gauntlet, and a challenge was born.

Now a home project, once the basic frame was intact, I enlisted my mom to drive me to the local welding shop where I somehow talked one of the grizzled gents into allowing me into the workshop. Working side by side with this pro welder, I arranged my bits of tubing and bolts using the wooden jigs I'd prepared so that the axle arms and spindles were just right. I managed to get the negative camber and caster—two things you couldn't be without—aligned as my new shop buddy made these parts permanent.

Somehow, there's only one photo of my go-kart. The chain isn't even in place yet, but the savvy '70s go-kart aficionado will note my homemade racing-style "butterfly" steering wheel and foot pedals. I may not have had the funds or the skill, but I was determined to make my kart look as close as possible to the real thing, right down to the racing decals and three-color paint job.

Besides the Stingray bike that we wild-at-heart boys had to have back in the late '60s, my first set of wheels was that go-kart. What an amazing moment, having the petrol-soaked freedom to drive—actually drive—a motorized vehicle. Forget all the good educational and character-building benefits of making your own kart versus the easy life of someone buying you a kart. It was the speed, the smell, the road two inches below, zooming by as I raced along, that tattooed my brain with a new sense of achievement. Sliding on sand and puddles and learning the basics of opposite-lock skid control took me to a whole new world, the world of speed, guts, and glory.

Of course, there was no way my parents would allow me to start my kart without first having a helmet. They were being typical safety conscious parents. Against all odds, I was actually dying for a real, honest-to-goodness racing helmet. Twenty dollars at Barker's for an Easy Rider imitation Stars and Stripes helmet. I wore that thing out of the store. I probably slept in it. It was just the coolest. Of course, along with the safety gear came the endless reminders from my dad that I was not to drive that thing on the road. Yeah, yeah, sure, sure . . .

Next up was even wilder. I was poring over a *Popular Mechanics* magazine from the school library and found an article written, it seemed, just for me: *Build Your Own Hydroplane*. Wow! I was a boater from an early age, so what could be better than traveling fast without rules or speed limits? Now thirteen, I dreamed big and proceeded to talk my mom into driving me to Torno Lumber for some critical materials.

I can't imagine the harebrained story I concocted to convince my mom to pay for a couple sheets of marine plywood, assorted pine boards, glue, and screws. This, I guess, was my first experience recruiting an investor to fund my dream. This dream just happened to come from two small pages torn from a magazine.

I quickly converted half our garage into the Wiener Boat Werks and got down to making the coolest speedboat any kid could imagine. I learned about waterproof glues and fiberglass resins by first slopping them all over my clothes, wondering what I had bitten off. Fast-forward to the fateful launch, where it was almost curtains for yours truly.

My boating life to that point consisted of racing sailboats on the open waters of Long Island Sound so that was my territory, and as any self-respecting hydroplane racer would know, rough, salty water is far from ideal and potentially deadly. So what? I had to make my maiden voyage. It was late afternoon on a blustery fall day. I powered out of the marina with an anemic, four-horsepower Evinrude to my vast "test track" beyond the breakwater and land, battling into wind and waves that were better suited to late-season bluefishing and big-boat sailing. Before long, I was swamped. With no one around and far from shore, I had to weigh my chances: pull the drain plug in the stern, power along, hoping physics would allow the drain plug to work as designed, or drift helplessly and hope for a passing fisherman before sinking.

I took another risk and quite literally pulled the plug. Thankfully, physics prevailed, the seawater slowly drained out, and I made it back to port completely soaked, scared, but alive. Putting all the fear and danger behind me, I later talked my friend, Chris Olson, into installing his fifteen-horsepower motor on my craft so we could see what real speed on the water felt like. That ended after about thirty seconds when the boat flipped over thanks to all that awesome power. I just wish I had pictures.

My first business, at thirteen, also revolved around the boating life. I got talked into cleaning the bottom of a big sailboat—while it was in the water. Seemed nutty at first, but then it made sense: if you want a competitive advantage in sailboat racing, clean the slime and goop off the bottom of your boat. Thus my first business was born. This unplanned business emerged courtesy of a bunch of guys who were petrified at the thought of anyone having a slight advantage.

Cleaning algae, and in the worst cases, barnacles, off big, beautiful boats was a messy, dirty business, equal parts gross and creepy. Add that you are a natural bobber with limited lung capacity, trying to brace yourself against something you've already concluded is super slippery, and suddenly this isn't some recreational swim at the beach club. No, this is work swimming, and you have to do it, rain or shine. Thirty- to fifty-foot boats take a long time to clean properly, especially when one breath allows you just enough time to swim down, brace yourself, and take a few quick swipes at the slime and sea-glop before racing to the surface for air.

I eventually graduated from a snorkel to an old air compressor, and I instantly increased my efficiency. At times, it was scary swimming for hours in the dark, all alone, wondering about sea monsters, sharks, eels, and other imaginary dangers. I kept plugging away, knowing I was earning money and feeling like a salty business tycoon.

With visions of expanding my boat-cleaning empire, I tried my hand at marketing for the first time, not that I knew to call it that. I wrote up a sales flyer with pricing based on different boat lengths and got it copied at the local print shop. I laid my flyer in the cockpits of every big boat at the yacht club and waited for the phone to ring off the hook.

Bad luck. The weather turned ugly the day after I'd placed all my flyers. It rained buckets. I got phone calls. They were not for new business. They were irate boat owners complaining that my coated Xerox paper came apart when wet, leaving melted, white cornflakes all over the place. Major setback and time waster, but I learned a valuable lesson about another unknown: product liability. This incident taught me the importance of thinking things through and trying to predict how a product might get used and abused. Many years later, I'd park a Range Rover on top of our commercial outdoor speaker product to ensure its durability, create a sensational sales photo, and avoid liability claims from theme parks.

I spent the next few days cleaning up boat cockpits and apologizing to people I'd never met. The good news was my repair effort and responsibility resulted in a number of new customers. Hmm . . . young David learns Business Lesson #7: admit you were wrong, be responsible, fix the problem, and win customers.

It's just too bad people back then didn't take countless photos like they do today. It would be fun to see pictures of me in my underwater glory, along with my friend and first "employee," Robert Davidson, who convinced me to share the two-piece wetsuit I'd invested in. Think Laurel and Hardy meet the creature from the Black Lagoon.

The saltwater life wasn't all work. Risk has no mercy on the immature, and we tested this theory endlessly. When I say we, it was often me and my two friends, Scott Reichhelm and Robert. We found all manner of stupid things to try, and the fact that we spent a good part of our lives on the water meant we had limitless possibilities—and no speed limits. We'd prove our bravery—and contempt for Davy Jones—on rough waters by *jumping* my family's motorboat over the biggest waves we could find. Robert, Scott, and I would stand side by side and hang on to whatever we could as we hurled the boat into the air at insane speeds. Sadly, our adventures in stunt boating came to an abrupt end one day when, with Robert at the wheel, we targeted one of the many large rectangular box-shaped buoys used for the club's sailing races and regattas. Our spectacular trajectory and subsequent flight of destruction eliminated all traces of the mark, leaving us feeling pretty guilty, as our families were longtime competitors who had raced around the club's buoys for many years. OK, only a little guilty, and mostly exhilarated, so in typical teenage-troublemaker fashion, we swore each other to secrecy—something I'd be doing more than once in the coming years.

In junior high, I pointed my photography hobby toward those things that interested me, namely sports and action, influenced to a great degree by "assisting" family friend and legendary *Life* photographer, George Silk. Soon I was selling boat photos to local yacht racers, shooting by day and developing film by night in my darkroom (really the laundry room). I would spend whole days down there on weekends or summer days off. I was so into it that I'd lose all sense of time. It was only when my mother would bang on the door with "Dinner is ready" that I'd awaken from my creative stupor and realize I'd forgotten to eat all day. (Up to her last days, my mom loved to remind me of those times and punctuated most of our phone calls with "And don't forget to eat!")

Losing all sense of time is a recurrent theme. As my career progressed, I realized there's a critical balancing act one must play in order not to completely sacrifice family, friends, and fun for your business. That doesn't mean it's fifty-fifty all the time. It's not even close, but a little sanity and balance is a good thing. Being an entrepreneur is a way of life; it's not something you can leave behind when you close the door to your office. It is the uninvited guest sitting at your dinner table, sleeping in your bed, accompanying you at your kid's sporting events, and owning more of your mind and heart than you will ever confess.

I worked hard at photography and got serious, peddling photos to editors at magazines in New York City. I would walk into their offices, large portfolio in hand, and talk them into meeting with me to review my work. These excursions to editors were, in the truest sense, cold calls. I'd take the train into Manhattan, as I was too young to drive, and hit any office I could get into (the only way their doors opened was by my knocking on them).

New York City was also the site of my camera-repair gurus—Professional Camera Repair and the incomparable Marty Forscher—so I had more reasons to be in Manhattan, particularly because I was doing things like mounting my motorized Nikon to my skis and racing down Stratton Mountain in hopes of capturing unique images, much to Marty's chagrin.

In an odd evolution of risk and skiing, years later, I would bolt my ski bindings to the roof of my car and clamp in while my employee Billy Bob drove like a bat out of hell so I could train for speed-skiing competitions. Maybe the boat thing wasn't so outrageous ...

I was sixteen when I truly turned pro. Midway through dinner one school night during tenth grade, the phone rang. My mom handed me the receiver. It was highly unusual to get phone calls around dinnertime, and interrupting a meal for a call wasn't popular in our home. The stranger on the other end introduced himself as Bob Tringali, verified I was "the David Wiener, sports photographer," and proceeded to explain that his agency, Focus On Sports, had seen my work and wanted to represent me. Now, imagine you're a kid and you get asked to sign with an agent. I was floored. It took all of my being, as my family watched, to stay somewhat calm and agree to meet in New York City to walk through the opportunities and money that were about to come my way.

Shooting professionally for *Forbes*, *Newsweek*, *Time-Life*, *Yachting*, *Yacht Racing*, *Sailing*, and many others, I became the youngest photographer ever to work the Indy 500, the US Open Tennis Championships, the America's Cup, and many other events. I quickly discovered that being the youngest, by a good margin, had its benefits, and I put my talents at talking my way into things to the test, including convincing the center court umpire at the US Open to let me sit beside Bjorn Borg and Jimmy Connors so I could get closer to the action during their matches. All the seasoned pros had to remain behind the Photo Media lines wide of the court. My young age and the fact that I was an energized, trim, blond kid set me apart from many of the overweight pros with their fishing vests full of gear, their floppy sun hats, and a seeming sense of bored resignation, given they were likely shooting the exact same photos as the guys next to them. The Monday following the tennis finals, all the excitement of my center court treatment was further enhanced when kids at school said, "Hey, Wiener, we saw you on TV at the US Open!"

Another unbelievable moment was when I shot the ultimate sailboat race, the America's Cup: the United States versus Australia. It was 1974, and I was on assignment at sixteen. I had my driver's license, but the ink was barely dry, and I'd never driven more than an hour from home by myself. This was a maiden voyage on all fronts.

The first day was amazing: eight hours shooting the coolest sailboats, riding on the most luxurious motor yacht I'd ever seen, an elegant lunch onboard, and me, the only photographer on the boat. I was feeling pretty big-time as we motored back to port, towing the sleek US boat, *Courageous*, and her crew—a post-race tradition allowing the team to organize the boat and pretend to relax a bit.

Later I met up with the Southern Cross team, my hosts for the next couple of days. I'd never spent time with real live Aussies, and I quickly embraced their good nature and enthusiasm for everything, including my being the youngest person they'd encountered working the Cup. They made it their mission to "educate" me on a whole bunch of things, especially beer. Getting plied with endless John Courage Draft would have been thrilling for any underage drinker, but better than that, I was treated like one of the team.

The following day was nonstop shooting from their tender, another elegant motor yacht. I was fed and watered like a VIP. And it got better. I was invited to hang out with the team and was immediately accepted as an honorary member when they discovered my willingness and mechanical aptitude to help them tweak their boat for the next day of racing. I was amazed at how much this level of yacht racing resembled Formula One car racing. They pulled the boats out of the water every night and got down to making serious alterations and adjustments—major tweaks. The first project was extending the keel using two giant aluminum plates. This was serious surgery, and I was right in the middle of it all, behind giant curtains to keep out prying eyes. Tools in hand, bloody knuckles, and all. I was one of them. It was great. After the keel, we got down to recutting sails, trimming, and sewing them on a huge sail-loft floor, which resembled a gymnasium with a single sewing machine sunk in a hole in the middle. I was helping and learning all at the same time.

Their level of commitment and energy astounded me. I had a sense of belonging to something serious. Something big. At the same time, I couldn't help feeling conflicted about helping the competition. After all, I was an American at the America's Cup. But I got over it. This team was so committed and so fun—and there was so much beer! When it was all over for the night, we drank Courage like a bunch of high schoolers at a Friday night party. I enjoyed my assignment and raised my professional credibility all at the same time. Too bad my teachers didn't give grades for that.

Who knew the bar would just keep rising? In 1976, as a high school senior, I was called to shoot the Indianapolis 500—a dream assignment that would open my eyes to no shortage of crazy. I convinced my parents that missing some school in May during my "senior slump" semester wouldn't have any negative impact on my education. In fact, just the opposite! This would be the biggest road trip of my life, and I'd do it with my friend and newly minted photographer's assistant, Sean Doyle.

Doyley and I set off for Indy early one weekday morning, arriving outside the track that evening, thinking life couldn't get any better. Little did we know. A little while later, a cute woman in a Datsun 240Z pulled up and invited us to a party. Smart high schoolers that we were, we said yes! Once at her condo, we came to realize *we* were going to be the party—and her birthday present. She had scoped us out and decided we were perfect for her one-night sexual fantasy adventure. She worked me over, then Doyley, then repeat. Doyley and I spent much of the time looking over at each other, grinning with looks of *Can this really be happening? Are we really this lucky? It's just the first day!* Hours later, Doyley and I were swearing each other to secrecy as we drove off, fearing our parents—and all of Westport—might hear about our unbelievable exploits.

The next day felt just a bit anticlimactic, and it was Indy, baby. Friggin' Indy! That's just crazy. The mad adventures of Davey and Doyley hit the rev limiter the night before, and it would be a long time before it would become any less of a sensational moment. But now it was time to work, be professional, and get the shots.

I went about my business shooting the Indy 500 from every angle, and as usual, getting as close as possible always: Gasoline Alley, the drivers' meeting, the starting grid, the pole position holder, Johnny Rutherford, and the assorted cast of supporting characters. I was closer to the action than I had ever imagined, inside with the likes of Mario Andretti, A. J. Foyt, and the rest of the speed merchants.

I finished out the multiday assignment, giving Kodak stock an uptick, and we drove home to Westport, burnt to a crisp and wondering how we would face regular life at school after our eye-opener at Indy. How would we face our parents? Our friends? Girlfriends our own age? We had committed ourselves to total secrecy. That lasted about a week.

The stories leaked out, and to this day, our friends still demand retellings of what happened at Indy. I guess Doyley and I really were that lucky!

I was a determined kid. Long before I got my license, I loved cars, and I really loved Porsches. I told anyone who'd listen that I was going to buy a Porsche. Didn't matter that I wasn't even legal driving age, I still broached the subject with my dad. After all, I was a hardworking, ambitious guy, and I was committed. More like, I should have *been* committed. My dad immediately responded with this mind-numbing statement: "Kids don't need cars, and any car you get you have to pay for yourself, and it has to be a wreck so you can learn to fix it, and then you have to sell it. *Because kids don't need cars!*"

OK, so there was that. Now how to skirt around this edict? First thing: get a car. No—get a Porsche.

I was pretty creative about earning money, and when it came to my dream car, nothing was beneath me. I was sixteen when my car mission turned serious. I was selling my photography to magazines and individuals, but that wasn't enough. I needed more immediate cash. Business Lesson #23: I didn't consider that all the minimum-wage, hourly work I could dig up was nowhere near as lucrative as selling a unique skill—in my case, sports photography. No matter, I was determined, and hourly work provided a warped sense of instant financial gratification.

I started down the usual route high school boys travel. My first minimum-wage job was dishwasher in a restaurant with food so sketchy I was constantly confronted with half-eaten lobsters, and had a daily struggle with myself about whether to snack off the plates on the conveyor. It wasn't long before I quit and got a job as a busboy at a much nicer spot. Next, I got a job as a personal shopper and house cleaner for a family friend whose wife had just given birth and couldn't do the work herself.

Bonus round: I got to drive her stick-shift Fiat to do the grocery shopping. Race Car Driver Training 101! Next, I talked my mother into letting me wash the windows on our house for $75. Then I sold anything I had to help fund my dream. I even sold my prized Fender Jaguar guitar, then my Fender Pro Reverb amp. That was dumb.

As an adult, I'd have many similar experiences trying to find money to fund my work dreams, both courting investors and selling prized possessions to ensure I'd meet payroll and get to the finish line. I never had the benefit of crowdfunding platforms like Kickstarter, where you can use the power of the internet to expose your ideas and raise money without giving away equity. That would've been a game changer for me. But a word of caution: far too many crowdfunding campaigns have successfully raised funding using pretty pictures and cool videos, but they have no idea how to actually manufacture and deliver the products they are selling. Please, if you go this route, make sure you can deliver.

As I hoarded money for my dream Porsche, I began my hunt. I scoured the car section of the classifieds. Mind you, I didn't have a solid budget, but I figured I could amass $1,500 or so if I worked like a fiend. That's not a lot of money when your taste runs to exotic foreign metal, but oh well. I wanted a Porsche, still I was open-minded and realistic about my budget, so I looked at anything that even slightly reeked of Euro cool. Of course, I never mentioned any of this to my dad.

I looked at an XKE Jaguar. I looked at a Fiat 124 Spider. Next up, a Triumph GT6. I started learning about how one buys a used car: I made an appointment at the local Mobil station to have a proper mechanic look it over. The crusty mechanic took one look at the GT6 and blurted out, "Gee, your girlfriend's parents will be thrilled when they see a car this small. You can't get in any trouble in that!" I didn't need his views on my dating adventures. Just clam up and check out the car! It didn't end well.

Dejected at the terrible options available to a car-mad kid with limited funds, I was close to giving up when I happened to accompany my mom to a foreign car repair shop in Norwalk where she was having her car tuned up. I was wandering around the storage lot outside, and there it was. The car gods were smiling on me, rewarding my patience. I spied a tired-looking Porsche in a sea of foreign beaters. I went inside, found the owner, Larry Prentiss, and got a quick education in buying a hammered Porsche. He could sense the total passion and commitment in me and took pity, offering me the car for slightly more than my growing budget, along with the promise of answering questions that would arise as I took this car from thrashed to something better. Then he lowered the boom, explaining that the car barely ran and would need an immediate engine rebuild. "But you can handle it if you get a good manual and make the occasional phone call." Sure, no problem.

This would turn out to be a life-defining moment for me in so many ways. The car was a 1966 Porsche 912, a four-cylinder version of the more potent and classic 911. Same body, same suspension, but a simpler motor that would be far easier for me to work on. It was chocolate brown with terrible paint and a worn out interior—but it was a Porsche. It had that iconic profile, racing heritage, mythic performance (in my head), and classic smell.

I went back some weeks later with my money and took delivery of one, very old, very used, much-in-need-of-help Porsche. I was over the moon. I got in, started it up—and it sounded awful. But I did as Larry instructed: "Drive straight home and no further, or it may blow." I was insane with delight and lugged this thing the three miles home, but like any self-respecting would-be Le Mans racer, I decided I had to fly this machine to the far end of our road. I sped along and promptly encountered the stone wall at the end of the lane, skidding to a stop only inches away, unaware of all the sand that had collected on the asphalt. With my heart in my mouth and pride on hold, I crawled home and parked the car in the driveway in order to give it a thorough wash and cleaning. I lathered and washed and scrubbed and vacuumed and polished and poked and eventually stood back to admire the first Porsche ever to grace our driveway. It would be hard to concentrate in school the next day.

Of course, every honeymoon comes to an end, and mine ended twenty-four hours later. I went to the local foreign car parts store after school and got a Porsche repair manual. The chapter on engine removal was daunting, and I wondered just how over my head I'd gotten. No one I knew had ever removed an engine.

I took my manual to school the next day and sat through an endless series of boring classes, waiting for the final bell to ring. The school bus doors were barely open when I jumped out and ran down the driveway to begin surgery.

The next many weeks were a blur of bloody knuckles, greasy fingernails, and far too few correct tools as I disassembled and rebuilt the engine. But I was thrilled. I had worked on a real live Porsche motor. I'd held all sorts of odd and intriguing parts, kept them in order (as the book admonished), and put the whole mess back together.

But I was far from done. I had to fix the body's dents and bruises, then repaint the car, and then do something about the interior. No small list of things to learn and tackle. Enter Dwight Bell, high school senior, owner of a Triumph TR6, and my tutor on bodywork. He taught me a valuable lesson: Bondo. That magical body putty would be my friend, and it could fix or cover up any combination of ills on a car. I got right into it.

As my project progressed, my dad, who had gotten over the shock of finding a Porsche at home, poked his head into the carport at different times and mentioned that he had a spray gun that would work off the same compressor I had used to breathe underwater. He also inferred that he was quite the expert and that he could spray my car. Wow, an instant ability to paint cars! It had never occurred to me that it could be this easy—or that the compressor was totally wrong for the job. I pored over paint chip catalogs at the local body shop supplier and finally, after endlessly changing my mind, bought a gallon of metallic dark green. Not a Porsche color, but I hadn't yet learned the concept of using *only* Porsche paints to keep things kosher among the cognoscenti. Let's call it innovating.

Amid this marathon project, I managed to hone my amateur race driver skills anytime I could sneak out my mom's Mercedes sedan. It was a big, lumbering thing that was more elegance than get-up-and-go, but I managed to slide it around turns and scare the piss out of myself on more than one occasion. The best one was the time I spun it on Imperial Avenue and ended up with phone pole splinters sticking out of the wheel-tire seam. I was so lucky that was the worst of it, and that none of my family ever knew anything about that one!

I soon learned a few more valuable lessons: *you get what you pay for, don't believe claims,* and *ask to see samples.* We are all tempted by the easy way out, the shortcuts, the cheapest option. Invariably in business, any one of these typically leads to disaster. But I was a kid, stupid and excited. A free spray by my dad was priced just right.

I did all the body prep, hundreds of hours of sanding, all the masking, paint mixing, and all the other labor. Then my dad waltzed in and sprayed the paint—damn the few runs and drips (maybe no one would notice). I reinstalled the motor, then the interior I'd fixed and dyed. I affixed all the body trim I'd repaired and even pushed the limits of my enthusiasm and knowledge by painting the chrome window frames flat black—"Just like the *new* Porsches!" Going even further overboard, I made a dashboard panel with ten—count 'em, ten—cool toggle switches. I wanted James Bond mixed with an F-16. It looked great, even though most of the switches weren't connected to anything.

I kept my eye on the prize: driving my own car . . . a Porsche. It was beyond amazing on that fateful Friday night to have the engine solidly back in the car. Naturally, I had chosen to delay going out to the usual Friday night high school parties in favor of getting my car to run. I'd spent all afternoon and evening getting things put back together, and wired and sorted, and finally I was ready for the big moment. Thankfully, Scott and Robert, who'd lived through many of my insane projects, showed up to provide moral support and then drag me off to the night's parties.

With a crazy mixture of fear and confidence, I turned the key and cranked the engine. We were silent, holding our breath. After multiple tries, mostly to get fuel flowing to the carburetors, there was that sound of ignition and then burbling. We had liftoff! The thing worked. It was truly one of those great achievement moments, though one mostly celebrated in my head, as others would never know the amount of work, focus, learning, fear, toil, and blood—real blood—that was behind this one moment.

About this time, I had to face my dad's kids-don't-need-cars attitude and devised multiple arguments to convince him there was simply no way I was selling this laboratory on wheels, this mobile classroom, this precollege PhD in all things mechanical—this hot, hot car. For once, school came to the rescue.

As seemed standard operating procedure by now, I bit off more than I could chew with a major media class project. Better to dream big or not at all. Instead of the typical written report or collage of pictures torn from magazines, I chose to make a Porsche commercial, using 16-millimeter film to create a "professional" piece to impress my teacher and classmates. I had never shot a film, and I had no idea how to thread a movie camera, edit film, create a soundtrack, or put it all together, but I borrowed a camera and rudimentary editing gear (two hand-crank film spools, a mylar tape splicing guide, and a cassette recorder), and ultimately wowed the class. It felt so pro, though watching it today makes me cringe. But hey, Dad: look at all I am learning!

My rolling lab became an endless experiment in body, paint, and interior redos. When the Porsche performance catalogs started filling my family's mailbox, I was in heaven, reading every page the way I had drooled over Fender guitar catalogs in elementary school. These automotive bibles were chock-full of the fiberglass fender flares, wings, air dams, and engine parts the guys on the world's racetracks were running. As funds permitted, I transformed my car with wider fenders, wheels, and tires, an outrageous homebuilt air dam, and more. I did the painting this time, choosing classic gloss black to show off every curve I had painstakingly caressed with endless sheets of sandpaper to get them perfect. I knew a real paint job would highlight even the smallest flaw, so I spent the time on prep. A lesson for the future, but not one that stuck too quickly. Just ask my high school friend, Freddy Meyers, whose Triumph Spitfire went from mustard to drippy metallic silver. (I hadn't yet learned that metallic paints are heavy and more prone to drips). What a complete mess I made of that!

The real turning point in my car mania came when the father of a high school friend saw what I was doing and asked me to create a custom

Porsche for him. He was a doctor, had the dough, and wanted a cool car. He'd pay for the car, for all the coolest add-ons—and for me to build it. Pay me? A high schooler? This was the beginning of something great, and a precursor to one of my first *real* businesses a few years later.

The car thing went on and on. Along the way, I developed a reputation within the local Porsche community. After college, I started building custom Porsches. I was approached by car magazines like *Motor Trend*, customers from both coasts, and even George Barris, California's king of custom and creator of such masterpieces as the Batmobile, the Munster's Coach, and many more. He sent customers my way, having seen and read about my work. I was learning by doing.

As a driven kid, and as an entrepreneur, designer, and at times, salesperson, the skill of talking people into things was, and is, a critical talent required on an almost daily basis. My first car proved this. The power of talk is something they don't teach in college MBA and entrepreneurship programs. I think it's learned in the field. Early in my career, I bought an audiotape package offering negotiating skills, yet I can't remember a single thing it taught other than the term *gambit*. Gambit? Seriously? What are we, Vegas sharks? Go learn it the old-fashioned way. Get out in the trenches and do it yourself. Get off email and learn to speak to people. Be compelling. Make them want to ask questions and realize your dream with you.

After high school, I would learn more things that weren't in any textbook. Powered by a warped self-confidence, I figured I could do anything I wanted, and I did! Almost . . .

CHAPTER 3

SCHOOL'S OUT, THEN IT'S BACK IN

CONSIDERING ALL THE WILD AND INSANE capers during my high school years, it was nothing short of miraculous I graduated ready for college. Well . . .

As a high school senior, I went through all the motions of applying to college, thinking photography would be my major. I did the interviews, showed my portfolio, and got accepted into some of the best university photo programs. The question I had to ask myself: Why *study* photography when I was already accomplished at doing it? I could head to *Sports Illustrated*, be their youngest-ever photographer, and have a good job and no shortage of excitement. Trouble was, I realized I had a bigger passion than photography: mechanics, cars, and creative invention.

I knew it was too late to apply all over again for the coming school year, so I battled myself to figure out what I should do: take the easy road and accept my place in one of the country's most respected photography programs or throw it all to the wind and hit restart.

I took a big breath and approached my dad. I explained my thought process and my idea to take a year off, apply to engineering schools, and make the most of the next twelve months. It didn't go well, and of course he had his opinion on the subject, one I had never even considered. "Engineering is such a sellout. Why would you want to be an engineer?"

After lots of back-and-forth, I finally got the green light to take the year off. I passed on the acceptances I'd received and started planning, and since applications wouldn't be due for many months, I had time to think about and do other things. I spoke to family friend John Cuccio, who was painfully aware of my love of cars, racing, Ferraris, and mechanical things, having witnessed my go-kart and hydroplane escapades. As the local *Tifosi*, I asked him countless questions about his Ferrari 275 GTB and 365 Daytona. Mr. Cuccio had created a successful industrial design business in Westport, which only added to the intrigue for me. After a conversation about my plans for the upcoming year and beyond, he told me two things: "First, you will not spend the year working at the body shop you mentioned. You will become a designer to develop your talents. Second, travel to Europe, and I will write a letter of introduction to Ferrari to enhance your knowledge of cars and design."

I managed to find the world's cheapest ticket to Europe, my mission to visit the critical sources of automotive history—namely, Porsche, Ferrari, and BMW. In Stuttgart, I talked my way into Porsche's secretive racing department, showing photos of my handiwork to ensure they understood my level of Porsche insanity. I also showed assorted drawings I'd made of new and novel performance accessories and installations I had in mind for the 911. This was the late '70s, so I was there when Porsche was winning everywhere with the cars I dreamed about. Of course, I had to tempt fate and immaturely risk it all before leaving.

Visiting the Porsche Museum (much different and smaller than the one that exists today), I spotted the most potent Porsche of all. The most impressive race car of all. The legend. Mark Donohue's world-beating Sunoco Porsche 917. I abandoned all reason and conveniently forgot the admonishment my parents had told me a thousand times: "Don't touch the art." But you understand, I had to touch it. Better, I had to assume the position. What might it feel like to sit in the seat that Mark Donohue himself had sat in as he went on to win so many races in this monster? I handed my Nikon to my friend and made it clear to him that this was going to be an action shot—I was going to be in that car for the briefest of moments, so he'd better not screw it up. I was in and out before the guard, sitting just around the corner, could register what was going on!

In Munich, I got a tour of the BMW factory and left with a sense of what real manufacturing and automotive production could be. Totally different from the small numbers at Porsche. On to Italy!

For some, the Vatican, Israel, or Mecca represent the ultimate spiritual experience. For me, Ferrari induces that truly religious experience, as everyone in Italy knows and understands. I got on a bus in Bologna aimed in the general direction of Maranello. I had no real idea where I was going or how exactly to get there. I didn't speak Italian, and my high school French was useless with the bus driver. An idea—I pulled out the sealed letter Mr. Cuccio had given me weeks earlier. Though the paper was wrinkled and maybe even a bit smelly from a life inside my nomadic backpack, I showed the driver the envelope with the word *Ferrari* printed on it. A broad smile flashed across his face, and he blurted out, "Niki Lauda! You Niki Lauda!" I was saved. He understood exactly where I was headed and pulled the bus to a stop sometime later, right in front of the famous gate that signals the entrance to the Ferrari factory. Thank goodness, because as anyone who has traveled to Maranello can attest, the town is tiny, and that gate, along with the entire factory, can be missed in an eyeblink.

I thanked the driver and the entire busload, all of them smiling for me, and descended to the gate. I must have been a sight, carrying all my belongings on my back, dressed in basic clothes and no hint of Italian style. I signaled the guard, who spoke less English than I spoke Italian, and slipped the letter through the gate, hoping there was truly something magical in its content. The guard huddled with his sidekick and a moment later opened the large sliding gate, motioning for me to wait in the guardhouse. At this point, I had no idea what might come and wondered if my long Italian adventure to reach Maranello had been for naught.

After fifteen minutes, a handsomely dressed executive type strolled in, introduced himself, and treated me like I was a visiting prince. Thank you, Mr. Cuccio, for an experience I will never forget! Nowadays, it takes high-level clearance to get inside the racing facilities at the factory. The same held true in 1976, but I got in—everywhere—and toured the engine foundry where workers poured molten aluminum from handheld crucibles. (Today it's done with assorted robotics and conveyors.) Next was the Formula One shop where the cars for the global superstar Niki Lauda and his teammate, Carlos Reutemann, were being assembled. I had died and gone to heaven and I got my first real taste of what being a VIP meant (as it applied to a scruffy American tourist kid). Having returned to the Ferrari factory many times, I am always reminded of how the factory has grown and how that guardhouse is now a proper building.

But the nostalgia is intact, as the entrance gate and entry archway have remained almost unchanged.

There was a lot more to absorb during my Euro travels, but I left with my interest in making things mechanical cemented, riveted, and glued firmly in place. I was going to study engineering!

Back home from Europe, I got a job at a local company, Cambridge Research, which specialized in taking new product concepts to market. Seemed like the perfect place for a kid wanting to get into engineering, design, and such. The partners of the company pegged me as both a lackey and a car "expert," leaving me to fix things around the office, run errands, and thankfully, drive and wash their fleet of cool cars. The job went well, and I was the only kid in town picking up his girlfriend at the high school in a stunning Ferrari Dino one day, a Pantera the next, and a Porsche 911—the real thing—the next. It was insane. I'd look for any excuse to *need* to drive somewhere. All that exotic sheet metal made me want to raise the bar on my own car.

After building and then rebuilding my old Porsche 912, I figured it was time for the big leagues. I'd cut my teeth and proven my worthiness. I was ready for it: a 911. That was the serious rig. The sublime motor. The big horsepower. Racing power. A 911 also meant serious expense. I once again went into money-saving mode. I did all the last tweaks I could think of on the 912 and readied it for sale. I then hunted down the lowest-cost 911 I could find, which is a dangerous thing. As I'd learned with my dad's paint spraying, you get what you pay for.

One car sold and another purchased, I was back to square one. Clean, strip, disassemble, fix, assemble, cut, rivet, weld, fill, sand, paint. Thrilling. This went on every free moment I had, which translates to nights, weekends, and holidays. When I wasn't at work, the dinner table, or my girlfriend's house, I was in the carport getting greasy and bloody, or I was in the basement fabricating wings and fiberglassing them until the entire house was toxic.

After many months and using up every dollar I'd earned, I had the meanest, coolest 911 I could imagine (well, with imagination on a budget). I finished the car about the same time I was accepting my admission to the engineering school at the University of Vermont (UVM). My possibilities for Porsche improvements would be unlimited once I had real engineering knowledge. My diabolical plan was moving forward.

The one sensible thought in my head was that there was no way I'd be taking this 911 to college. See, there was a glimmer of hope for me being reasonable! No one at UVM would understand that I'd built this car, that Daddy didn't buy it for me. This car was just too outrageous, and as cool as it was, it would be totally uncool to show up at school with this thing.

Beyond obvious jealousy and other hater behaviors, I learned something big just days after finishing the car, when my new creation was keyed in a Westport parking lot while I was out on a date. The spineless worm hit every panel. After my initial nuclear meltdown (internal as to not freak out my girlfriend), I learned a valuable life lesson that night, though I didn't realize it for a couple of weeks: Life is short. Don't let the many setbacks I'm headed for derail me at a moment's notice. Maintain perspective when the going gets tough. It's not cancer, it won't kill you. It's just metal and paint and time, and time does, in fact, heal all. This was a lot to digest, but it had a big impact on me. I answer many problems that arise in my own family now with "No one died," hoping to impart a sense of perspective to any disaster du jour.

The black 911 cemented my status as a custom Porsche builder. Over time, I'd continue on the path, selling and leveraging the sale of each car to up the ante, buying an even better "foundation car" for my next experiments. Build, show, sell, buy. Build, show, sell, buy . . .

My year off taught me some important life and business lessons, but getting into a college had been overriding all other thoughts. When I applied to UVM for the 1977 school year, it was so popular they didn't allow interviews for the sanity of their admissions personnel. But given my lack of academic inspiration in high school, my grades weren't going to get me in, so I drove the five hours to Burlington and talked my way into the admissions office for an interview. Thankfully, my passion and portfolios of car design and professional photography showed them how committed I could be when driven by personal desire. I was accepted into mechanical engineering, much to my dad's chagrin. It was almost impossible for me to understand how he could be so negative. Luckily, I'd become used to it, so I just focused on my path.

I figured that having *real* engineering knowledge would support all the crazy projects I had in mind—and might eventually get me into a Formula One team over in England, the hub of all things F1. Although I loved UVM and Vermont, six months in I saw a different picture, a bigger one: the dream. My dream. Sure, I was going to miss my friends, the cute girls, and the great town, but I knew I needed something more to round out my skill set. I needed to combine engineering with more freedom to experiment and, at the same time, add in a heavy dose of art and sculpture so I could draw and model my experiments. I also needed to tie in the study of aerodynamics, for obvious reasons. Hampshire College (and the four other colleges in the Five College Consortium available to any student at Hampshire, Amherst, UMass, Smith, and Holyoke) was a better fit. I applied, was accepted, decided to transfer for sophomore year, and told my parents—all in that order.

I would spend the next three years taking art and design classes at Hampshire, engineering and aerodynamics courses at UMass, and sculpture courses at Smith and Holyoke. I planned to maximize my opportunity in Amherst, but first, a summer job . . .

Having survived my freshman year of UVM engineering and knowing I would be transferring to Hampshire in the fall, I headed home and immediately got a summer job at the famed Chinetti Ferrari in Greenwich, headquarters of the equally famous North American Racing Team, known the world over as NART, Ferrari's US motorsports operation. I would be working under Nereo Iori, the most respected Ferrari race mechanic in America. I didn't realize it at the time, but it sure makes sense to work for the best possible talent or teacher you can find. Like so many things, it sounds obvious, but how many people actually search out great talent to work for when summer job hunting? In fact, why is the obvious not always obvious? This is an interesting concept and one that I would interrogate many years later as part of my Future Review management concept, which helps predict problems and mistakes before they happen. Sometimes, we're just too close and need to take that critical step back to see the forest for the trees.

I worked as Iori's assistant (*apprentice* in Ferrari racing culture), building race engines. My first assignment was rebuilding a distributor, and I quickly realized Iori spoke slightly more English than I spoke Italian, which was limited to a collection of curse words. We developed our communication based on a variety of facial expressions and wild hand gestures. But we made it work.

It was in the Ferrari race shop that I learned a valuable lesson about tools—and the size of my arm. There's a joke that goes, *The human arm doesn't have enough elbows to work on a Ferrari motor.* What I discovered was the concept of *building* your own tools—taking existing wrenches, for example, and then cutting, extending, adding bends, and welding the whole mess back together, allowing the critical end to snake down into the depths of the engine compartment and do its one specialized job. It had never occurred to me to purposely cut up a perfectly good wrench. An aha moment: you can make anything you need to make the making easier. Funny that I had no qualms about cutting a Porsche, but I found cutting perfectly good tools somehow disrespectful. That didn't last long.

My next project was line boring a twelve-cylinder race engine to ensure that the crankshaft and bearings fit perfectly—and by perfectly, I mean I had to endlessly assemble the bearings, along with a solid, heavy precision rod of steel, along with polishing compound inside the crankcase of the engine. Torquing the many bolts to exact specs, I would then spend ten to fifteen minutes spinning the rod from one end, using a smaller steel rod as my T-handle. It was painstaking. After taking it all apart, I had to clean all the parts and reassemble the whole thing with a small piece of thin putty, torquing it all down just so. Then I'd take it all apart again and measure the squished putty using a micrometer. Doing this repeatedly, we could measure exactly how much more polishing (microscopic metal removal) needed to be done. We did this over and over and over for days on end.

My position as Iori's apprentice allowed me certain elevated treatment compared to the "regular" Ferrari mechanics who worked on the GT customer cars out in the main shop. It also allowed me to pull a David once in a while, like the time I took one of the GT cars for a test-drive around Greenwich after repairing something that surely needed to be performance tested. That didn't go over so well with the service manager.

My work with Iori also led me to meet the infamous Coco Chinetti, son of the legendary Luigi, the original importer and distributor of Ferraris in America and a celebrated Le Mans winner. Coco was a well-known fast-living playboy whose bad-boy image, combined with his race-winning talent, made him a walking spotlight everywhere he went, from Le Mans to Lime Rock. It was Coco who, a year later, would ask me to manage the Ferrari display at the New York Auto Show. Amazing. To be asked by a growing Ferrari legend to single-handedly oversee an exhibition as critical as the New York show, with Niki Lauda's F1 World Championship car and other equally important and valuable machines under my watch—I felt like the king of the car world as I stood behind the red velveteen ropes keeping gawking visitors from drooling on these precious works of automotive art. I'd reconnect with Coco decades later while exhibiting a luxury David Wiener Ventures product we made in partnership with Ferrari. It was great to see him, laugh about the past, and hear more of his hijinks. What a memorable summer job and the subsequent opportunities it created. I was part of something that meant so much to me and opened doors—and still does.

Studying engineering, art, and aerodynamics at Hampshire and the surrounding colleges gave me a great academic foundation to build upon. I also learned some early lessons about creative businesses and being an entrepreneur. I treated college like it was my personal experiment and laboratory for all manner of ideas, designs, prototypes, and a bit of academics. Given my natural tendencies toward racing cars and the technology of Formula One, I was gearing up to create some kind of amazing vehicle for my senior thesis. I wondered what I could possibly do. What I could possibly afford. What I could possibly graduate with. I had two years to come up with a plan.

Naturally, along the path of all this experimentation and thinking, I also managed to have some wild times—a few even involving engineering and problem-solving. Like the time my friend Matt Balk and I found an aboveground swimming pool at a local yard sale and decided we could buy it and install it *inside* our dorm lounge. Thankfully, somewhere between counting out the hundred dollars the farmer wanted and beginning to disassemble the monster, I suddenly considered the physics of a full twenty-foot-diameter pool sitting in a fourth-floor room. Visions of us creating a twenty-foot donut hole through three suspended floors and being dragged off to jail collided, flipping a switch in my brain. We politely asked for our money back and quickly exited, but the risky business followed me.

On the slightly more controlled side of college life, risk was my entry into national presidential politics. More accurately, I went to hear presidential candidate Congressman John Anderson at a campaign event at Amherst College (I was attempting to expand my universe). Unfortunately, when my friend Joel Roos and I arrived at the auditorium, it was packed to the gills. Totally claustrophobic. I ducked backstage in hopes of finding some place to sit. Then the opportunity presented itself: I simply walked by everyone, strode out onto the stage, and plopped down in one of the two elegant armchairs set stage right of the podium. I just sat there and tried not to make eye contact with anyone too official looking. I got a lot of odd looks but none as odd as when the security detail walked Mrs. Anderson out to seat her next to me. Thankfully, they didn't want to upset her by creating a stir, so I got to spend the time chit-chatting with the candidate's wife as if we were in our own little world. A few minutes later, John Anderson took the stage, gave his wife (and me) a quick wave, and went on to deliver his stump speech. For my part,

I just sat still, smiled, and gave his wife the occasional nod of approval. Joel was in shock, but by this point, he was almost used to my antics, after assorted parties at Smith College, car races on the back roads of Amherst, and other ballyhoo.

The best part was weeks later when my father asked me if I had been to a John Anderson campaign stop. Apparently a number of his friends had been watching *60 Minutes* and called my dad to say they had seen me sitting on stage with the candidate during a segment on Congressman Anderson. Maybe that would impress him.

Along with a variety of summer jobs, the gas crisis of 1979 provided an opportunity for some impromptu entrepreneurial adventures as I, along with my friends Sean Doyle (Indy!) and Jack Petropoulos, dove into the coffee-and-donuts business, planning to assault the miles-long gas lines at the Westport Mobil station. It was a perfect captive audience, entrepreneurship without even knowing it was happening. We just agreed we'd get "the stuff" and hit the gas lines by six the next morning. We mixed comedy with sales and walked away with real cash and some hysterical stories of early-morning encounters. We did this a few times, but it was short-lived, as we all had to get back to school.

The college engineering study and experiments eventually led me to my senior thesis. I knew I couldn't build a race car, so I throttled back and decided to design a vehicle to race in the Human Powered World Speed Championships, another potential stepping stone on my path to automotive design. What I hadn't realized at the time was that this thesis would require me to find sponsors, raise money, talk suppliers into providing free materials, and figure out how to get this circus from Amherst to Pomona, California, for the World Championship race event that May. It was all pretty entrepreneurial, though I had no idea at the time. Keeping me in check was the weekly reminder that the previous year's champion was a multi-engineer, professional team from the giant defense contractor General Dynamics. And in case that wasn't enough to scare me, some of the other teams I'd be competing against included multistudent teams from top engineering schools like Cal Poly. I was probably the first-ever one-man (student) competitor to attempt this challenge. And it got worse.

Along the way, I tested the limits of my capacity to bend the rules. This included sneaking into the University of Massachusetts machine shop and learning how to use their Bridgeport milling machine to make the giant gears required for a world-record bike. I also talked my way into the president of Hampshire College's office to use their phones to hunt for sponsors, even convincing them to lend me a spare office and type letters for me! It was about this time that someone in their office nicknamed me Golden Tongue. The pressure mounted daily. I secured sponsorship from Campagnolo, the legendary Italian bike components company, as well as DuPont, Celanese, North Sails, WonderKnit, and Adidas. I also raised funds from sponsors, two college grants, and a few extended family members.

A word on raising money: it's not easy—or it wasn't back in 1980. I had to go out, like a beginner start-up, and beg for dollars. I sent a staggering number of letters—real letters, no email—to seventy large corporations: McDonald's, Boeing, IBM, Ford, and more. Total struggle, especially as I was supposed to be doing the actual *work* of designing and engineering a vehicle, figuring out how to build it, and doing everything related to that. My thesis would be graded on design and engineering, not on money and sponsors.

Raising money generally sucks. It's hard, often demeaning, and always stressful. You will be tested, challenged, and tortured with endless questions, often from people with no clue what they are talking about. But they have the money, and you don't. With the often-reported news these days of venture fund investments in tech, software, app, and social media companies and lifestyle, yoga, essential oil, and CBD start-ups, it's easy to think that funds just fall off trees. The reality is this: most people never get funded. Of the ones who do, they often have to sign away huge percentages of their companies. These days it's a bit easier, but back then it was really hard. No email, no PowerPoint, no Zoom meetings with angel investors across the country. Hell, no computers—and long-distance phoning was expensive! The takeaway? Be careful when you go hunting for funds. Be sure you are truly and fully committed. Be sure you really can't find the funds elsewhere, and be sure you raise enough. There's no room for optimism when creating budgets for a new venture (or a thesis project!). It's all daunting at best. Bottom line, and the real reason I was able to complete the project—a project everyone believed far too big for only eight months—was my total commitment and unwillingness to hear the word *no*.

So there I was, about halfway through the school year, and deep into all the work and stress of trying to survive biting off way more than I could chew. I was so focused on building the world's fastest bike that I hadn't given much thought to who would ride the thing, but suddenly it became the issue du jour. Add yet one more huge challenge to my long list.

After endless worrying all by myself, I figured I'd enlist a little help. Very little. I sat down at one of my usual cafeteria lunch tables, surrounded by a cast of characters that included some bike-racer types. I started moaning about who was I going to get to ride my bike. After a bit of jawboning, one of the guys joked, "Why don't you get Eric Heiden to ride the thing." Everyone laughed. I didn't. Eric had just become a household name as the greatest Winter Olympian ever. He'd achieved the impossible and won all five speed-skating golds at the 1980 Lake Placid Games. The entire free world knew who he was. They knew where he lived, his father's name—everything. That's what instant fame and exposure will do for you. Just the info I needed.

Taking a leap, I phoned Information, got the number, and called Eric's family home. I had no idea what I was doing, and I didn't know Dr. Jack Heiden or any of the Heiden family, but I figured I had nothing to lose. Thankfully, the stars aligned, and Eric answered the phone. (I later learned that the good doctor Jack, had he answered, would have told me to piss off, though in a polite Midwestern manner.)

Eric and I hit it off immediately, as he was totally intrigued by the idea of seeing how fast he could go on a "bike." Words like *cool* and *definitely* peppered the conversation. He told me I'd need to clear it with his agent, but he was totally psyched. I was on cloud nine. I couldn't wait to tell the guys. They'd never believe it!

Working with Eric's agent was a different story. Art Kaminsky was a tough, professional New York agent, and he didn't relish some college kid possibly killing his prized client in a world speed record attempt. It took a lot of calls, a couple of meetings, and a lot of pressure from Eric to convince Kaminski and company not to charge me for the opportunity to turn Eric into a speeding missile, or quite possibly, a crash test dummy.

I'd finally gotten past this hurdle of legal and contractual fencing and then it got more interesting. Eric let me know he'd be flying through JFK, heading from one major event to another. This would be the only window of time when we could meet in person, take measurements, fit Eric to a wooden mock-up of the machine I had designed, and figure out as much as possible during his one-hour layover. Oh, and Art would be traveling with him. Hmm.

My college friend, Zippy Zimicki, and I drove to New York from Amherst and proceeded to carry an eight-foot-long contraption, tools, cameras, and more through JFK and into the international lounge. It being 1981, my science project seemed utterly uninteresting to the guards, the security, unlike today, being far less demanding. We did attract a fair bit of attention though once Eric stepped out of his pants and into a pair of training shorts to better allow for exact fitments, measurements, and photos for later analysis.

As we worked away, Art couldn't help but be petrified. When he saw what I had in mind for his superstar, he voiced his concerns and stated Eric should not have any part in this madcap adventure. Art lost. I won.

A month or so later, I was on a call with one of my sponsors. He said he'd like to ride my vehicle at the World Speed Championships. His name was John Howard, and he managed the sponsored athletes and programs for the vaunted Campagnolo. "Campy" in the '70s and '80s was considered the *ne plus ultra* of the bicycle world. Worth its weight in gold, the gear Howard sent me was amazing. He was a friendly older guy who kept the boxes coming, but when he suggested he could ride my bike, I felt like I'd been put in a very awkward position.

At my next lunch gathering in the cafeteria, I mentioned this turn of events to my biker friends, telling them that this character, John Howard, wanted to ride *my* bike. I was hoping for some advice on how to brush him off. Instead, I got this: "Are you kidding? Do you know who John Howard is? He's only a major Olympic bike racer, and he's just won the Ironman Triathlon in Hawaii!" Wish I'd had Google back then.

Months of intense days and little sleep resulted in a truly exciting and hugely difficult last year of college, rife with terminal stress, crazy moments, and experiences that would shape my future. About five months in, and just when I thought things couldn't get any weirder, PBS contacted me to say they'd heard about my David-versus-Goliath challenge and wanted to make a documentary about what I was doing. The immediate thrill of in-depth television coverage quickly gave way to new stress, as every detail of my project would be dissected for the world to see in living color, not to mention the constant event coverage when my twenty-hour days were punctuated with in-depth interviews morning and night. Stress in its purest form: not enough time and too many distractions. During one of their interviews, I actually found I had one ear focused on the interviewer while the other ear was listening to my responses. I wondered if I was making any sense to the PBS crew during that, my first and only out-of-body experience. I felt like I was floating above looking down, watching and listening to the interview. Bizarre. Maybe it was just the lack of sleep.

After eight months of sleepless nights, extraordinary stress, and a Herculean effort, I was a week away from the World Championships in California. I'd done everything I possibly could to achieve my goal, including arranging for *two* bikes to be shipped to California, where I'd meet them along with a few students I'd chosen to be my pit crew, mental support, and general safety net. But at that moment, I had to pack the bikes into crates and drive them from Amherst to Boston's Logan Airport.

My Hampshire twin brother from another mother, Matt Polstein, volunteered to drive, knowing I was an exhausted bag of bones. He drove the rented truck loaded with my two monster crates as I tried to sleep, my nerves shot. My only sense of peace was that I'd convinced the airfreight giant Flying Tigers to ship the crates for a heavily discounted price, important as I was running out of money.

After a two-hour drive late at night, we pulled into the airport's commercial freight area and proceeded into the gigantic Flying Tigers hangar. We hunted for the right person to speak with and quickly discovered that they would ship the crates but that it would cost thousands more than had been discussed. They demanded payment in advance, and I did not own a credit card. There was no time to spare and no money to begin to cover this insane charge. That's when my nerves finally snapped. I was crazed, exhausted, almost delirious—and mad. I wanted blood.

Matt knew me well from all our college and kayak-racing adventures and wanted to avoid an explosion. He quickly took charge, pushing me onto a nearby chair while he pleaded my case and explained just how much had been invested and how much was at stake. I mentioned he was my "twin"—well, it turns out he was quite the talker and quite convincing. When he came to gather me up from my funk, he informed me that Flying Tigers would like to be a sponsor and that they would fly both crates round trip for free, and all I'd have to do is plaster some of their decals on my bikes and sew patches on our uniforms. This was such a shocking and welcome bit of news that my exhaustion seemed to immediately subside.

Needless to say, the World Speed Championships were a mixture of excitement, frustration, success, failure, and crazy moments, all rolled into a five-day marathon. Due to an army-like adherence to their schedule, the event organizers denied us additional speed runs to see what the terminal velocity of my lightweight machine was. Eric kept going faster and getting more comfortable with each run and told me he hadn't even started to really push it. When Eric Heiden says that, you believe him. So frustrating for Team Wiener—but at least we'd shown well and attracted a ton of spectators to the event. As a stress release at the final ceremonial party, Eric and I instigated a food fight just to remind everyone that this was supposed to be fun!

The takeaway from this project was priceless knowledge that I would build upon in subsequent ventures. We didn't win, but it was one of the most amazing experiences I had ever been through.

Returning to school, with graduation a couple of weeks later, I experienced the highs and lows of being a student celebrity. With television news reporters attending my graduation, I felt both accomplished and embarrassed. I had achieved something big, and yet I recognized other students with important projects that didn't get any attention, while I was being interviewed on camera in front of the entire graduation audience. My feeling that I was getting too much attention served as a helping of self-imposed humble pie to give my ego a reality check.

While I cannot emphasize enough that we should savor each victory, there is a huge caveat. Don't believe all your own press. Remember, fame really does last for only fifteen minutes before the next news story hits. When projects are lauded, we can quickly become legends in our own minds. The danger here is losing that self-analytic criticism so important to pushing the limits and creating the best possible ideas and products. I think the excessive criticism I was raised on helped prevent my basking in the rays of my graduation and PBS glow. This, mixed with the fact that I hadn't achieved the level of success I had set for myself in the race, meant the glow was dramatically dimmed in my mind, regardless of what professors, friends, and the press had to say. Whether facing a performance issue—or in later years, a sales issue—I have always been my own toughest critic, and I don't let the highs allow me to forget the lows. It only took another thirty-five years for me to learn to celebrate the highs.

As I've said for many years, fake it till you make it. Whether it's convincing people that you belong at that VIP event or you need them to sponsor your work, it's all the same. It's about deciding that you belong. That you've earned your spot. That you have a good reason for what you are trying to pull off. Be compelling. Be convincing. My postcollege experience would test this practice in so many ways, as I'd soon face everything from vendors to lawyers to magazines and TV journalists. I was about to leap into a much bigger fire.

CHAPTER 4
COLLEGE GRADUATE

I WAS OUT. A GRADUATE. Twenty-three. Nothing tying me down. Independent. Now what? Well, like plenty of other twenty-three-year-olds who graduate with no resume or job prospects, I moved back in with Mom. For a week. Yes, just a week. I needed to stow my stuff, party with my high school buds, and eat some good home cooking, but I knew this wasn't going to last long, especially with my father pushing me to join the Peace Corps. Sheesh, did he even know me?

I worked construction in Vermont for a couple months and visited girlfriends on Cape Cod. Then I decided Boston might be a good place to find a first job. That happened—sort of. I found an apartment outside Cambridge and tried to figure out next steps. Little did I know that within a month of moving I'd be catapulted back into my thesis.

While I was wandering Boston one day, learning my way around a city that clearly gave no real thought to how the streets were laid out, I ended up at MIT: the hallowed grounds of engineering, technology's

Mount Olympus. There I was, viewing the elegant display cases chock-full of MIT miracles and feeling academically insignificant, when I stumbled upon the highlighted, newest hot project of the MIT mechanical engineering department: my thesis! It was a true double-take moment. Picture after picture of me, my bikes, my riders, and my team all labeled as if it were MIT student work. I was pretty shocked but still innocent enough to wonder how this happened. Something was fishy. I did some investigating, asked around, and found the lab where a team of MIT classes was working on an odd four-rider speed bike. Big mistake. Maybe they weren't yet engineering gods. Turns out some of the photographers hovering around us at the World Speed Championships were actually MIT engineering students with phony 'PRESS' emblazoned on their hats. Impressive—they had nothing to show for their efforts, so they used photos of my work to tell their story!

After thirty days of wandering (and wondering) around Boston, I met my first real boss. Dr. Paul MacCready was a legendary engineer in the aviation and aerospace world and the recipient of hundreds of awards, including the American Society of Mechanical Engineers' Engineer of the Century award, seven honorary degrees, Aviation Week's Aerospace Laureate designation, and California Institute of Technology's Graduate of the Decade award, and *four* Kremer Prizes for engineering. Google him.

I met Paul MacCready at a lecture he gave at MIT. I knew of Paul from his lofty position as president of the World Human Powered Vehicle Association, which presided over the World Speed Championships that I had recently competed in. To hear him speak at MIT would be a thrill. The god of vehicle innovation, he'd worked extensively on human- and solar-powered aircraft. Imagine a human-powered aircraft light enough for a single rider to pedal and fly across the English Channel. Not satisfied with doing just that, he created a solar plane that flew 163 miles from France to England. He also created vehicles for GM along with many other innovative products.

After his lecture, I asked Paul to sign my copy of his book. That meeting led to an extended conversation and an invitation to breakfast the next morning. My first business breakfast! With a legend! Wow. Paul asked lots of questions, got a sense of my drive, and in an amusing turn, asked if he could use my dad as a reference, as he believed fathers were very respectable agents of information (and since I didn't have a lot of references yet). I was excited and nervous. He got on the phone with my dad. He hung up and offered me a job on the spot, telling me to get to California immediately. I needed to pack up and get moving. Having just settled into my first-ever apartment (and lease), this came as quite a shock, but I realized how important this opportunity could be for my future. We cemented the offer and arrangements. I packed up my apartment, stuffed my car, and drove to Simi Valley in record time. (Special thanks to Jack P. for taking over the lease!)

I quickly became engulfed in a project Paul had with Huffy Bicycles, the world's largest bike manufacturer at the time. He was to create the next-generation bicycle, and I would be part of the development team. It didn't take me long to realize that the team's focus on innovation far outweighed the desire to create a truly commercial vehicle that the public would want and embrace. I liked the idea of innovating and creating something unique, but I knew enough to realize our grand creation had to appeal to the people who vote with dollars: customers. As time ticked away toward the big unveiling two months on, I kept trying to inject bits of design and style into the vehicles. By showtime, I had become thoroughly frustrated, realizing that all the powerful creativity and engineering talent in that facility was going to go down in flames because the vehicles to be presented were hideous—more experiments in drive-train mechanisms than inspiring and salable creations you could enjoy riding. They looked like prototypes Dr. Frankenstein had made out of junk parts.

Finally, after a late night of last-minute adjustments and preparations, it was time. Two Huffy execs showed up the next morning and were led to the shop's back lot, where we had the prototype vehicles on display. Let me paint the picture: two husky guys in gray suits and ties staring at three mechanical contraptions that looked like bad metal shop projects, our crew of four people, and Paul MacCready, genius. It wasn't going to be pretty. The two execs pondered the "bikes," probably wondering if the rattle-can paint was dry or if the bizarre chains and springs and other assorted "features" were going to ruin their fine clothes. After some coaxing, they climbed aboard to test-drive these bikes of the future.

Were they entertained, amused, or embarrassed? Bemused and maybe even a bit scared was what I saw. They did figure eights and other maneuvers, getting comfortable with lever steering, lean steering, and under-seat steering, all without an accident or torn pant leg. They dismounted, made some comments, and that's about all. There would be no giant contract. I was embarrassed, more for Paul than anything. His amazing ability to dream up an engineering wonder seemed to have overshadowed the needs of a consumer-market product. Huffy left without a bike that screamed, "I'm your new bestseller—the way of the future!" We were left with three oddball vehicles no self-respecting cyclist would want to use.

Frustrated with the attitude about the project, the prototypes, and the presentation, I told Paul I was going to leave and start my own company. He took it well, understanding the power and passion of the inventor spirit. He wished me great success. I packed up my little car and pointed it east. Next stop, Westport, Connecticut. Once again, I was on a mission: get back as fast as possible to a place where I could start creating all the things I had been dreaming up. The sky was the limit, I had my pay, some graduation money, and the future seemed bright.

Years later, having created many successful products, prototypes, and presentations, I became even more aware of just how flawed that Huffy project was. There was little to no real agreement on what the products should have been, or how to execute them in a manner that would have shown their effectiveness and wow the client. While many engineers never consider image and marketing or pooh-pooh it as nonsense, there is simply no reason to make the mistake of assuming an idea is so good and powerful that it will be instantly accepted, warts and all.

Think about professional auto-racing teams as an illustration: even the last-place performers prepare and polish their cars and dress their crew to look like front-row winners. Why? To build team morale, but more critically, to get the best response from potential sponsors and the media, which translates to income, the key to staying in business.

By the time I got back to Westport, I was absorbed with the idea of starting a company and pushing my ideas out to the world. I wasn't sure how I would do this, but I knew I would. I rented a house and moved in with a mattress and a selection of kitchen odds and ends. I needed a place to eat, sleep, work, and store stuff. Given my aesthetic demands, I wanted to create Wiener World as I saw it. Necessity is the mother of all invention, and I swear it's true. Without one stick of furniture, I became very inventive.

I turned every room except the kitchen and my bedroom into a workshop. I laid down plastic sheeting and plywood on the floors, built four-foot-by-eight-foot worktables, and got to it. Naturally, I didn't mention this to my new landlords—they seemed pretty uptight and likely wouldn't have considered me a fit tenant had they known my demented plan for their house.

I set up a workshop for "dirty" work in the basement, complete with a worktable, a bandsaw, and a whole bunch of hand tools. The question that nagged me: How could I eliminate the time waste and frustration of shop cleanup when it was far more important to be dreaming up the next project or racing out to some social encounter?

The self-cleaning workbench was an obvious solution, and it all came about when I was at one of my many favorite places, the local hardware store. I spotted a roll of bungee cord, and it hit me: if I hung all my tools from the ceiling using bungee cord, I could simply reach up, grab a tool, use it, and just release it when done. Presto! There'd never be a tool lingering or littering my worktable. Turns out this was a really dumb idea, as screwdrivers and other tools became lethal weapons as they were released, but I tried.

I was determined to create unique designs. At the same time, I needed things to sell—and fast. I needed some reinforcement that my ideas weren't crazy. With all this in mind and knowing I needed to outfit some of the spaces in my rented house, I decided furniture and furnishings were a great outlet and source of potential customers. After all, modern furniture and lighting had become fashionable, and I was certain I could make things that people would want. It was almost like the elementary school days of creating something and then taking it around and seeing who might pay real cash for my creations.

I began collecting raw materials and hardware and got down to building a variety of modern lighting and furniture on a shoestring budget, using low-cost, high-tech materials and hardware found on Canal Street in New York City and assorted scrap yards, the gold standard of which was Vulcan Surplus in Stamford, just fifteen minutes from home. Vulcan was the dumping ground for all the technology manufacturers in Connecticut, providing mad inventors on a budget with everything from circuit boards to machined metal parts to aircraft components. I filled my car with a wild assortment of parts at a price that would have shocked the corporate CFOs who OK'd their original purchase. I would drive home thrilled at my amazing finds and great luck. This wasn't ten cents on the dollar—more like ten cents on a hundred dollars.

My living room quickly began to resemble a scene from *Star Wars*, with table legs made from concrete-filled rubber gloves, light fixtures made from plumbing valves, and speakers made from industrial vent hose (remember this one because it plays a major role years later). I created all sorts of odd and unusual furnishings that became my first products. Over time, using my old teenage photographer's method of just showing up, I'd go into Manhattan design showrooms to develop connections and representation for my furnishings. This didn't happen overnight, but with persistence and a series of increasingly unique furniture pieces, I started to build interest—and my bank account, which was a very good thing.

I plowed pretty much every dollar I could into new materials, new parts, and Oscar Mayer Wieners. I'm not kidding. I hadn't taken cooking very seriously to this point, given the easy living of growing up in my parent's house, where my mom's European cooking talents and my dad's

Cajun and seafood culinary treats reigned supreme. Due to my insane passion, work ethic, and desire not to waste time on food prep and dishwashing, I would simply boil a package of hot dogs for dinner—all ten! I'd plop them onto a plate with a pile of ketchup or mustard and eat them like carrot sticks, inhaling as I worked. Being a world-class hot dog lover, I thought this was pretty fantastic and good for my career. And no, I am not related to Oscar Mayer.

If you think ten hot dogs for dinner to save time is weird, consider the other methods I devised to save even more time. First, I figured that I could be even more efficient if I combined my morning shower with breakfast. I'd take a bowl of cereal into the shower and kill two birds with one stone. Hell, a little bit of watery overspray in your milk really isn't a big deal when you're in a hurry. Next, I figured that since my days were often filled with the dirty work of grinding metal, welding, and spraying paints, I could save time during my evening shower by catching up on the car, design, and engineering magazines that would pile up on my bedside table. This proved tougher than eating in the shower; magazines tend to get wet and limp if you aren't a speed reader. Don't report me.

My first furniture pieces were made mostly of wood and metal and tested physics at every turn. The cantilevered dining table, suspended bed, monolithic stereo tower, and flexible lighting challenged the imagination. In the end, these early pieces led me to rethink my material and design choices. Meanwhile, the Memphis furniture movement was just emerging with its outrageous postmodern pieces designed by an international collection of well-known artists, designers, and architects. These pieces were more sculpture than useful furnishings, but the lines, the colors, and the press it received made me think furniture could be a showcase, a way to tell the world what my design values were: performance and style. I liked and was jealous of the Memphis pieces, especially since they got so much press yet were products you could barely use. I wanted to make a statement: furniture can be modern *and* useful. Comfort, fit, and human factors (later known as ergonomics) all mattered to me. I wanted to make outrageous-looking pieces that also worked.

I dove in deeper, making a variety of tables, chairs, room dividers, and couches. My medium was glass, aluminum, and suede leather, with assorted heavy-duty hardware bits thrown in. A wheel from an airline stair ramp was the inspiration for one of my earliest wheelbarrow coffee tables, and that got me excited about the idea that furniture could move. Tables could roll, tabletops could tilt, chairs could flex, and lights could be bent to fit a need. I knew that these ideas of movement weren't novel, but I could apply them in novel ways. After all, how many tables have you seen with a twelve-inch, eighty-pound industrial wheel supporting one end?

After creating a few pieces, I moved into phase two: photograph the work to show and sell it. I tapped my photography skills in my role as chief documentarian and art director for my new company. I used any available backdrop, from Compo Beach to the local gravel pit to my own roof. I figured creative photos would be more interesting than seeing one of my furniture pieces in an average house. I also enlisted the talents of two studio photographer friends, Peter Orkin and Carmine Picarello. I was amazed at what these two could do with the lighting and seamless backdrops inside their huge studio. Back then, they shot on large-for-mat film. Such high-precision film and shooting required careful setup, metering, rearranging of lights and reflectors, and the tedious Polaroid test shots to see what the picture might actually look like.

Peter and Carmine's precision taught me an important lesson in marketing photography: check everything. Every little bit of junk on the ground, the hair on the model, a fold in a shirt, a shadow, a highlight—every little detail—will conspire to ruin what would otherwise be a perfectly usable photo. It's amazing how the excitement and emotion of seeing a good shot come together can blind you from seeing a cigarette butt or a leaf lying next to the model. Sounds absurd, but it's not. Of course, we didn't have Photoshop back then to clean things up.

Fast-forward a bit. I created more pieces, took more photos, and upped my promotional efforts in New York City to attract attention from magazines and showrooms. The hot design and furnishings editors were taking notice. I was featured on the cover page of the *New York Times* "Design" section one Thursday—the first time they ever showed the actual designer, and not just the products. *Metropolis* splashed my products on their cover and New York's *Village Voice* did a feature, as did a variety of others from Connecticut to California.

This exposure was amazing to me. Forget that I'd been the subject of a PBS documentary. So what? This was new. This was now! I loved it, and I was starting to get orders. With representation in New York, Dallas, San Francisco, and Paris showrooms, I had to expand.

Expansion meant a new focus on things like pricing and expenses, particularly miscellaneous costs that the creative person typically forgets about, such as shipping, packaging, insurance, tool wear, and so many other things that eat up profits. The big question I needed to be taped to the wall: Am I spending it faster than I am making it?

I hired my first employee, Sharon McClaskie, who kept things organized, and then a high school student (Billy Bob), who I taught to do some of the woodwork, sanding, laminate cutting, and assembly. Whether the bottom line was red or black, I bought into one theory: you have to spend money to make money, so I started doing some small but regular advertising, trying to gain even more business. I was learning about the advertising world and its many requirements, such as how to produce camera-ready art. It was exciting to see these small black-and-white ads showcasing my products in the cool furniture and design magazines, though my excitement was tempered by seeing all the other much larger ads that were in color. I could only afford black-and-white (not even an issue in today's digital world).

I began to get commissions, along with requests from my showrooms to create variations on some of my pieces. It seemed the interior designers who prowled these showrooms were like those people who can't order food off the menu—they want to create their own vision of your work. I wanted and needed the work, but I was still young and headstrong and felt my work was being altered for evil, so I learned to charge enough to placate my inner artiste. We called it an *FU quote* when a showroom would ask me to come up with a price to do a custom version, the thinking being, *I really don't want to do this, but if the buyer is crazy enough to pay this price, I'll happily oblige.* I'm not proud to admit this, though it was good compensation, and it taught me about the relative value of my work and my time.

It wasn't long before my pieces were being featured in shows, in exhibits, and on the pages of assorted magazines and the design annuals put out by various art book publishers. Unfortunately, about this time, I began doing my predictable "what's next?" act, feeling that furniture was fun but not feeding my fire—my need for movement, speed, and action. I had created highly unusual, modern pieces. They were accepted, people paid premium prices, and I was getting a little bit of a reputation in the New York design community. I even had Andy Warhol come up to me at one show event to talk. It didn't matter, though. I was a car guy. A speed merchant. I wanted to design vehicles, my true love. But how to do this? Jump ship just as I am getting noticed? I needed more of a challenge and an outlet for my ideas on aerodynamics, styling, and detail. High-performance cars were my calling. I can't remember if I ever considered the risk. I just acted.

Getting back to my car roots wasn't necessarily an easy thing. I had ideas for two different cars I wanted to build, but it would require a lot of work and some engineering I had never done before. Could I pull it off? Would they be showroom-perfect and convince potential customers that they were real? And oh yes, I didn't have the funds to just do it, so once again, I sold the car I had and used it to finance the purchase of two lesser cars.

Naturally, my years at college had augmented my ideas about what might be possible for my next custom Porsche project, and I bit off a big one, deciding to create a version of the then-popular and rare Turbo Porsche "Slope Nose" inspired by the 1976 Le Mans–winning Porsche 935. But the David Wiener Company version would have to be way more outrageous than simply a copy of what the factory offered. It would involve the entire body and be more aerodynamic, with front end, doors and rear fenders all shaped and flared as one to create a far more "slippery" shape. And to top it off, I decided to create one of the first 911 convertibles in the country, as Porsche had just launched their own, and I believed we could create something more streamlined.

The second car would be a BMW long-bed pickup truck that would also feature a removable Targa top. Of course, BMW didn't make pickups, so this would be a real head-turner if it was executed properly. It might also attract the attention of BMW and maybe even a design gig. Or it could all be a gigantic mistake.

In my typical fashion of shooting first and asking questions later, I figured if I could pull these two off, I'd cement my budding reputation as a custom car creator in the rarefied worlds of Porsche and BMW. These wouldn't just be tricked-out cars with cool stripes and paint. No, these would be totally custom-built cars meant to perform and attract stares wherever they went.

I set about hunting down the two donor cars—always one of the most fun parts of any car project. They weren't elegant, but they were perfectly usable cars: one, a used Porsche 911 Targa; the other, a used BMW 320i sedan. With the two cars secured, the design and fabrication could begin.

Long before this country learned the term *tuner car* from reality TV shows, I was doing the job by "cutting up perfectly good Porsches," as one of my friends liked to say. Based on my love affair with Porsches, you might think it was difficult for me to power saw my way through a 911. Sports coaches talk about using visualization to achieve performance goals. I used this same technique to achieve *excitement* goals. This is what drove me and still does. Fear is always there. Always. Even with total belief and engineering confidence, I always face the undercurrent of fear of failure. But the idea of creating something I find thrilling is the antidote to that fear, allowing me to not just brave but relish the unknown.

This would be the first time I needed to make structural engineering changes to a car—to two cars actually—and my plan was quite strategic. I'd reinforce the Porsche with welded-in plates to compensate for removing the Targa bar. I chose a Targa model because the chassis was already engineered for extra stiffness to combat the flexibility common in cars without a structural roof; on Targas, the entire roof comes off. I could then cut off the Targa bar (roll bar) and use it as a structural element on the BMW pickup truck. Of course, cutting the entire roof off "a perfectly good BMW" meant I'd be eliminating a major structural element that had been part of the original factory engineering effort to create a great-handling sports car. I'd have to re-engineer the chassis before taking a saw to that one. As in brain surgery, there was no room for "oops."

Adding to this already sizable two-car surgical risk, my working with such fine machines and making huge alterations led to no shortage of problems and mistakes. One was trusting a local welding shop to weld the engineered reinforcement plates and tubing I'd designed into each vehicle to ensure structural rigidity and eliminate any chassis twisting during high-performance driving. I had carefully planned everything out and riveted the reinforcing steel parts into place in both cars and then took the cars to the welding shop to make them permanent. Disregarding all my instructions, including "Do not put the BMW on a lift to weld the plates because the chassis will flex," they made some serious mistakes. Once all the welding was complete, the doors of the truck wouldn't open. Time to undo and re-do all that work. What a mess and a total waste of time.

Business Lesson #17: It's a rare vendor who makes a big mistake and admits it. Worse, the norm is that if they even attempt to repair what they've screwed up, they will be mad about it and convince themselves that it was really your fault. Worse still, their rework will likely not be of the highest quality. If you've already paid, their focus and sense of urgency will typically go in the toilet. Lesson learned: Get it right the first time. Babysit the big ones!

Once I got all that straightened out and began the major cutting, I bit off yet another big chunk and decided to swap the existing 911 engine with a newer, higher-performance 911 engine. I'd read about engine swapping and saw it as an outrageous challenge with amazing potential results—but I had no idea if I could pull it off. Of course, my new friend at *PAR*, the local used Porsche parts and motors business, said it would be easy! Easy. . .

At the same time, I performed my next surgery, cutting the back end off the BMW and extending it twelve inches to give the truck an effective and appropriate-looking bed. The fear-confidence cocktail swirled in my head. Who was I to cut the entire back end off a car? Not a minor bit of work, but in the end, it was worth all the nerves and trepidation as I took a saw to this elegant car, seeing in my mind how truly cool it would be someday.

My goal and driving force all along was the requirement that anything going out under my company's name—then changed to W^2—had to perform and look like it had been built by the factory. There was no room in my conjured world of high-profile projects for anything that looked even remotely homebuilt. An endless series of cut-weld-rivet-mold-fill-sand-paint adventures ensued, and in the end, I created two vehicles that the automotive press ate up. We were getting the exact reaction I'd wanted all along: "Wow, I didn't know BMW makes trucks!" "Porsche makes 935 convertibles? That's amazing!"

BMW even contacted me about the possibility of producing a sport pickup truck. Can you imagine my surprise and crazy excitement? A BMW truck! By me! That was more than I could fathom. After a few calls, the execs at BMW decided they were in the car business and not the truck business. My creation would not be getting the green light, but at least they noticed. This was real validation that I was doing something right. My automotive design was being noticed by people who mattered.

When finished, the Porsche went to a buyer in Seattle, and the BMW truck went to a Boston computer company that used it for trade shows, filling the bed with their products. Both were satisfying and successful projects and, of course, inspired the next W^2 car: a Turbo-bodied Porsche Targa.

Impressed by the BMW pickup truck, a yacht racing team commissioned W^2 to create a BMW stretch limo to get them from race to race. Photoshop and 3D computer modeling were still many years away, so I had to rely on cutting up and gluing images scoured from BMW brochures to create a composite image of the proposed limo. After committing to the project, the client had me locate a BMW to use as the foundation for the limo. With the car purchased (their money, not mine this time), I began to assess the significant engineering and fabrication requirements and build schedule. I was launching my future with some real statement products.

Some years back, I gave a talk to a university entrepreneurship program. After my talk, one of the students showed me his half-finished electric car project and proclaimed, "I'm building my brand with this project." I loved his enthusiasm, but I told him it might be best to see the result before staking his reputation and brand on the outcome. I'd hate to see a possible failure become his *brand*. This conversation made me reflect on my own adventures, and I wondered, *When did I develop my brand, or did I?* Even though I never put words to it, my brand and image were evolving. Of course, it helped that I always waited to see what the public reaction would be before making any claims. Thankfully, by design, all my work has revolved around exciting or high-profile projects, allowing my brand to evolve on its own.

Whether you choose to design your brand ahead of your business or just let it happen based on your actions, remember that customers are the ones who will ultimately decide what the brand is or isn't. We can try to manage perceptions, but customers are the ones who define a brand, so I will push the idea of authenticity—authenticity of character and work. It's the best way to try to maintain some semblance of control over the public's perception of your company and brand.

In today's start-up-crazed world, think about all the brands you are bombarded with on a weekly basis. Many seem to be all claims and image, with little real innovation, differentiation, performance, or quality to back up the marketing hype (or hyperbole). As an example, I recently ordered bottles of nonalcoholic bourbon and gin based solely on some slick digital marketing and claims, in hopes of reducing the intake of Manhattans and martinis at Dave's Place, my home bar). Silly me. These products were awful, and worse, they tasted nothing even remotely like whiskey or gin. But they had great marketing and ads all over the place!

In 1989, I got a call from Ben Cohen of Ben & Jerry's ice cream fame. That was a shock and a mystery. How did he know who I was, and why would he bother calling me? It turned out that Ben served on the Hampshire College board after I'd graduated, and he'd heard about my work. Ben tracked me down, told me they had a manufacturing problem, and asked me to come to Vermont to review their production line. They were concerned about the consistency of distribution of their mix-ins, those wonderful, tasty treats we all buy Ben & Jerry's for: chocolate chunks, pieces of Heath bar, cookie dough, and such. Apparently they took even distribution very seriously and enjoyed pretty good consistency, but when customers would call and complain about an oddly distributed pint, the bosses would get bummed out. After all, they were committed to customer happiness and fun, and what's more fun than ice cream?

Thus began a consulting project that put me in a position that would become a constant theme in my work: being hired for projects where I had no prior experience. Of course, I never let that stop me.

I arrived in Waterbury, Vermont, home of the Ben & Jerry's empire, and was immediately introduced to Ben, King of Ice Cream. He took me on a tour of the production line and let me view their highly innovative and technical methods—like dropping cartons of Heath bars from a ten-foot platform in order to get just the right random breakage for the pieces going into the ice cream. I got a view into Ben's character too. He was fanatical about ice cream and was constantly experimenting with new ideas and flavors. During the tour of his test area, he mixed something up and immediately thrust it in my face. "Try this!" It was like being with an XXL-sized kid. Pure passion, which is the main ingredient to entrepreneurial success.

I took notes, made sketches, and realized I could employ the experience I actually did have—an advanced understanding of aerodynamics, which I figured wasn't *totally* different from fluid dynamics. And I'd had a fluids course (and lots of time in whitewater kayaks), not to mention a summer internship doing wind tunnel testing for Air Shield, the leading truck aerodynamics manufacturer in the late '70s. You can see how all of this relates to the flow of tasty bits in ice cream . . .

I went back to my studio, did research, and pored through food production and hardware catalogs. In the end, I provided revised plumbing designs to reduce turbulation (chaotic flow) as the ice cream moved through the overhead pipes on its way to being poured into containers. All of this was meant to reduce the opportunity for mix-ins to get caught in a vortex that might keep them from flowing along in perfect harmony with the rest of their buddies. I liked to imagine I was helping make every container of Ben & Jerry's more enjoyable!

Getting to spend time with Ben Cohen reinforced in me that I should never outgrow childlike wonder and exuberance. Moreover, while Ben's passion for ice cream was evident through his incredible concoctions, his passion for customer happiness sank in and etched itself on my developing business mind.

My company was building a reputation for advanced creativity, which led to more exciting associations. We weren't looking for clients, as I wanted to focus on our own products, but the calls we did get were always interesting. That same year (1989), with no warning, Nike called and said they wanted me on a plane. What? Now? I had been sponsored in college by Adidas, and I still maintained my loyalty long after graduation, but working with Nike and taking a trip to Beaverton would no doubt be educational. I spent the long airplane ride having absolutely no idea what I was in for. Not a confidence-building moment.

Upon arrival at Nike HQ, I was ushered into a conference room by Tinker Hatfield, Nike's design guru and the project leader. Once seated, he presented me with what looked like 20 pages, give or take a few. A massive noncompete, nondisclosure agreement. How could I read this gobbledygook, much less make sense of it all, when everything was happening in real time and Tinker's team was assembled to meet with me? Sometimes in life and business you just have to cross your fingers and hope the other side is honest and ethical. I signed.

The Nike team proceeded to give me a tour, explaining their methodologies on design, prototyping, performance, and testing. It was a whirlwind, given how big the Nike facility was, even back then. We had lunch and got down to business. Top secret. Seriously.

The pages of that monster NDA were as much about secrecy as about copying. Their Nike Air shoe suspension system had been a huge hit, and they wanted to advance the tech with something new, called Tensile Air, later to be known as Zoom Air. We sat there and brainstormed for a long time, and the next day I left with orders to keep working on it. True to their credo, I was told to "Just do it!" These were more than just words to Nike and me. I was charged with providing ideas for a better way to create a shoe suspension system that had a controllable surface. (The standard Nike Air bladders would expand, like a beach ball when pressurized.) The goal for *Tensile Air* was to keep the top surface as planar (flat) as possible.

We did our work, providing ideas and designs, materials, and more, playing our small role in helping Tinker and Nike create what would become the next hit on their mission for world (sneaker) domination, making running, playing, and walking safer, healthier, and more comfortable. It was a long way from their waffle-iron-molded soles!

As I mentioned, I wear Adidas, not Nike. While Nike paid me, Adidas sponsored me. There is a critical difference. It's important to be loyal, to show those who support you that you don't forget. Same with DuPont. They were one of the sponsors of my college thesis. I still have leftover raw materials from forty years ago—Kevlar, Mylar, and other innovative performance products—and I plan to use them up. Loyalty. I feel the same way about the good investors in my projects—particularly the projects that didn't pay off the way I'd hoped. I keep these people in the back of my mind and want to reciprocate when that big payday happens and I can surprise them with a check in the mailbox. It's not required, and it's not part of investor expectations. But it's my expectation, and I want to show loyalty for those truly loyal supporters. I've done it before, and I'll do it again.

Anyway, this was just the beginning of the David Wiener Company adventure. Things were progressing. We were growing. The next years would severely test my resolve, perseverance, loyalties, and ability to overcome stress at work and at home. I was also overdue for financial success. Time to work even harder.

CHAPTER 5
GETTING SERIOUS

THOUGH I'D GOTTEN DEEP into furniture, cars, ice cream, sneakers, and other projects, the memories of my thesis were still fresh, with the two speed-record bikes on display in my living room. This constant visual reminder and the fact that I'd never really gotten a good ride kept nagging at me. I decided to have some fun, so one Sunday, I lashed them on top of my car and headed into New York City, destination Central Park. This was going to be a relaxed adventure, riding them just for fun, the first real fun I'd have with these machines since I embarked on that college journey. Boy, did I get blindsided as my entrepreneur membership card got punched—hard. Turns out the masses of bike riders in the park that Sunday loved my bikes. And why not? They were totally different, wild looking, and fast—really fast. They were so fast, in fact, that I could ride one while wearing street clothes and crush the Lycra-clad bike racers in Central Park. The problem was this: all the excitement led to a lot of people asking, "Where can I get one?" Then the real problem: my gears started to spin, and suddenly I was working on creating a consumer version of my high-speed machines.

I began developing a prototype using tubing I bought from a local Midas Muffler shop. It was a here-we-go-again moment. I was back into the recumbent bike thing. I used what I'd learned from my college work and made the new bikes lower, more comfortable, and more forgiving. It didn't hurt that my workshop-house was near the beach, allowing me instant access to a straight stretch of road that was crowded with sunbathers, walkers, and bikers—more people to expose to my latest product idea, which I named LandSpeeder. The result was a lot more "Where'd you get that thing? Gee, how much? Oh, can you make me one?" Market research, and all for free.

As an entrepreneur still unaware I was one, I had to get creative to fund my various projects concurrently. Serial entrepreneurs have an odd relationship with money. For me, it wasn't about earning a lot of money so I could put it in the bank. It was about earning enough money from one dream to fund the next one.

But there I was, with a new, big dream of manufacturing recumbent bikes, and I needed money to make it a reality. Always resourceful, I parlayed my car-building experiences into a portfolio of pictures and went to see the local experts in customizing cars—Gleisner Coachworks in Norwalk, Connecticut—figuring I might talk my way into some paid work. Ernest Gleisner had been trained in Europe and became one of the few custom car shops in the United States in the '80s with an actual assembly line, used to modify acres of new cars. His work also included bulletproof and bombproof limos for government officials, rock stars, and such. Gleisner recognized my over-the-top level of interest, excitement, and energy and immediately contracted me to create a one-off Pontiac Firebird. Heady times for a newbie surrounded by workshop bays full of cars with submachine guns, oil slick spray cans, shoot-through door panels, and Kevlar bombproofing. Surrounded by wild stuff most people would never encounter, I received an abbreviated education in both design and business, as well as a source of funds to fuel my own ventures.

Years after doing the project for Gleisner, I learned more about the man and his business. It surprised me that I had been so bold in not just pushing for work but also voicing my unfiltered opinion when Mr. Gleisner asked me about a new project they were doing for one of the Big Three (General Motors, Ford, and Chrysler). It was a decal job for a line of boring subcompacts that Detroit hoped could be made sexier by the low-cost application of some vinyl stripes and swirls. Gleisner had shown me a lot of respect by asking for my opinion and ideas to make it all come together. My response to Gleisner, a la Howard Roark from Ayn Rand's *The Fountainhead*: "Why would you waste your time trying to make an ugly car like this look better with some phony-baloney decals?" He was pretty shocked, though he respected my stance and commitment to authentic style and performance. Of course, I'm sure he proceeded to put some miscellaneous stripes on the cars and collect a huge fee. Even though he didn't use my "insight," I felt valued and respected thanks to his interest in my opinion, a tool I'd tuck away and remember to use with my own teams over the years. Meanwhile, I focused on the Firebird project and had dreamy visions of dollar bills.

During the LandSpeeder recumbent bike venture, it became obvious I was going to need a real building and not just a basement shop and a few bedroom workspaces. I hunted around, knowing I'd have to downsize my rental house and rent a real shop, all for roughly the same total budget—a tall order. I eventually found an old gas station in Westport that was being used as a storage unit by the local oil and heating company. The huge space was amazing, the glass doors would provide perfect display windows, and it even had the original hydraulic car lift. I convinced big Bill Gault at Gault Oil to rent it to me, and we made a deal on a handshake, as my Connecticut Yankee landlord believed a handshake was as good as any lawyer's paper.

It's amazing to think that back then some people still respected a handshake, especially when working with a budding twenty-something entrepreneur. I liked that at the time and still do, though after being burned by no shortage of people I trusted, there's no chance in hell I would now trust someone with a major deal based on a handshake. So how do I deal with agreements these days? With a written and signed document, preferably witnessed, to avoid anyone claiming anything unusual. It's just too easy—and too common—for people to shirk responsibility, renege on deals, and use their own selfish justification to convince themselves and their associates that their snaky behavior is correct. It's amazing how easy it is for people to brainwash themselves that they don't owe money, a full day's work, or even an honest answer.

Most of the time, when I've asked a borrower for repayment, I've been made to feel guilty. While this might sound naive, that simple piece of paper can save a lot of ruined friendships, family estrangements, and headaches. Memories are faulty, and so are we humans. A piece of paper memorializes the intent and understanding and can save a lot of grief, angst, and sleepless nights, as neither party can attempt to retranslate intentions or point fingers at misunderstandings. Contracts keep everyone honest, and anyone who doesn't want to sign an agreement before they borrow is showing their true colors. My roots may be Connecticut Yankee, but I've learned the hard way.

I was now the proud proprietor of an amazing space, though one coated in decades of gas station grease and grime. I was lucky enough to have a partner of sorts, my former girlfriend's dad, Jerry Ward. Jerry happily donated his time, treating this as a new hobby (he was excited by anything that involved tools). He joined me in the search and rescue of the shop space, renting a steam cleaner to spray the walls and ceiling, leaving us with a nice, clean facility. He also surprised me with a giant W^2 Design sign he made to hang over the shop's parapet. It made us feel official. The W^2 was a nod to Jerry; I wanted to include him, given all his support, hence the new w-squared company name hinting at Wiener and Ward—and it sounded cool. It also felt good to have an adult around with real enthusiasm! Sadly, I couldn't imagine my own dad showing this kind of support.

All that excitement quickly faded as the reality of the Landspeeder went from fun and simple to hard work and torture, partly due to my dear old Ferrari friend, Mr. Cuccio. He had seen the recumbent bikes I was creating and asked me if I'd considered the liability issues of selling a high-speed, low-slung, nearly-invisible-to-drivers bike. Huh? Had I? Of course I hadn't. He directed me to an engineering firm that he thought might prove invaluable by providing some accredited safety engineering knowledge for my designs.

This is when things got really serious. Until then, I had been welding prototype bikes together in my old basement shop, painting them with rattle cans, and bolting all the parts on myself. Suddenly, I was thrust into a new reality: meeting with real live engineers at a successful company. They were professionals with a serious shop and a lot of employees.

They listened to my story and goals and came back to me with a proposal to revise my design for increased safety and durability. Then they set the hook: an offer to manufacture the frames for me. Wow—and they claimed I could afford it. They made beautifully detailed blueprints and showed me all their safety additions and tooling fixture designs that would allow all these parts to be made with moon-shot precision. They added suspension, heavy-duty steering arms, more seat brackets, and many other over-designed parts, which they assured me would make the bike perfect—and perfectly safe.

It's so easy to get carried away, and I did. I was too blinded by the prospect of a true production bike to see through their flawed design ideas and manufacturing plans—and greed. I was being seduced by their expertise, their credibility, and their beautiful shop. I had no manufacturing experience. They acted like they had it all. *Someone save me* is the lesson here. The natural tendency of people selling anything—in this case, a service—is to think they possess superior talent that they can leverage to court the almighty dollar. The movie *Tucker* comes to mind, where a great and talented dreamer gets sucked in and controlled by an assigned board of directors that proudly present design changes that eliminate Tucker's innovations in favor of convention and old-school (dullard) thinking, dumbing down a unique product.

The "experts" I was stuck with created a vehicle that now weighed in at twice what I had created due to their excessive use of heavy-duty tubing and parts so thick you could run them over with a car (the car would suffer). They also magically raised their development costs on a regular basis and delivered the first frames months late—only a couple of weeks before our first scheduled trade show. The cost was now equal to the advertised retail price of the bike—and that was just for the frame! My LandSpeeder had become the LandBarge—a very expensive one.

Suddenly I was faced with multiple operational issues, a big fat bill from the engineering firm, and a shortage of bike frames, not to mention two minor details. We had to show up at the Indianapolis Motor Speedway for that year's World Speed Championships to race our new bikes and present them to the public, and then return to Connecticut a week later to get three LandSpeeders prepped and shipped to Las Vegas the next day for the big Interbike tradeshow. I had two employees: my right arm, Sharon, and my bike-racer friend from college, Pauly Rinehart. Add to them three high school students and a couple of junior high kids, and we had a crew committed to getting us to both events. We spent an insane amount of time bolting bikes together, adding on the various parts I'd had made elsewhere, and created two race vehicles with sleek fiberglass fairings for Indy. Later, we built three standard LandSpeeders and packed them into giant boxes for the trip to Vegas.

With the engineering bills eating at me, I got up my courage and borrowed $14,000 from my dad—the only time that would ever happen. I needed to pay my bills, and I needed to survive my dad's ensuing critique, but at least I could cover the first in a pile of big bills to keep the engineering firm from screaming.

Of course, there was more disaster and stress heading my way, first in the form of the fiberglass aerodynamic fairings designed to encapsulate the LandSpeeder bikes. Imagine making a torpedo-shaped missile big enough for a bike racer to get inside. This was a huge project that involved making a "buck"—the full-size model of the part to be molded—so we could then coat it with polyester primer, sand it to a mirror finish, and lovingly wax it to ensure the fiberglass we were going to wrap it in would release from the shape once dry. If that wasn't hard enough, we also had to make a mold for the windshield portion of this aerodynamic enclosure, then take that mold to a company that could heat a huge Plexiglas sheet and drape it over the mold to form the five-foot-long windscreen. An endless list of minor details and frustrations went along with making this giant piece of aerodynamic plastic, but the clincher was that I wanted our vehicles to look pro. This meant getting the fairings painted.

I went to my good friends at a local body shop who knew me from my Porsche projects and got them to spray the fairings glossy white. All of this was happening on an abbreviated (i.e., rushed) timeframe, which added a secondary level of stress to the entire adventure. Enter disaster number 13. I sent my loyal and hardworking (high school student) employee, Billy Bob, to fetch the fairings using my Chevy Blazer. He loaded the first of the two fairings into the open back of the Blazer and drove back to our shop. Two items to consider: Billy Bob was all of seventeen, and he was committed. The thing about being seventeen is that he hadn't developed much experience with hauling big things around, so he didn't bother tying the fairing down, and being committed meant that when he drove around a corner at the first intersection and the fairing started sliding out the back, he jumped out of the driver's seat and dove into the back to grab the front end of the ten-foot-long torpedo to keep it from getting damaged. You can guess the rest. He saved the fairing but plowed the Blazer into another car. Perfect!

The Indianapolis race and Vegas tradeshow saga was long, exciting, crazy, and hugely stressful. I'd had to choreograph many people, parts, crates, displays, and a pit crew, traveling from one end of the country to the other and back again, all while my brain—and bank account—burned over the pro engineers I was hostage to. I was a novice, but I wasn't a pushover, and my manufacturing and personnel management education got a big dose of do-or-die training over the next few weeks. First, I had to remind the engineering firm that we had a contract clearly stating the cost of the engineering, tooling, and most importantly, the frames. I also informed them that there was no possible way I could afford to pay their past-due bills, given how late they were with their first delivery. No frames equals no sales, so they'd have to wait, and they would have to honor the contract or not get paid at all. Plus, they'd have to streamline their production and hope I could generate real sales.

It quickly became clear they were intent on gouging me in every way possible. They would not honor the pricing, and they were unconcerned about their late deliveries. This was a clear breach of contract, even though I'd never heard this legal term, let alone had any experience with such things. Still, I knew I had to get out of there. But how? All the tooling and metal parts were in their shop. What to do? Time for true creativity.

Stress combined with someone else's sleaze can inspire some great revenge ideas. After consulting a lawyer friend and calculating my next move, I approached the engineering firm in the most businesslike manner I could muster and calmly explained that the only way I could pay them what was owed would be to sell the LandSpeeder company immediately and use the proceeds to pay off their bills. I also explained that I would have to create a compelling sales presentation, which meant I needed a professional studio photoshoot of the bikes, tooling, and fixtures. It was a hard sell, but ultimately their greed got the better of them, and they saw the wisdom of this thinking.

I arrived a few days later with a rented truck and three of my friends. We loaded the massive tooling, hydraulic bending machines, and bike frame parts into the truck, telling them we were off to the photo studio and would report back. First-rate acting for sure. It was far from easy, and all the while they had an air of nervousness watching the assets leaving their shop. I didn't let that slow us down—we got out of there as quickly as we could. The next day, my new lawyer sent them a letter explaining that they'd never see the tooling or another dollar. They had totally scammed me, and it wouldn't take a first-year law student to figure out those slimeballs parading around as engineers had blatantly breached every detail of our contract and put my new business in jeopardy. In the end, I think they had less manufacturing experience than I did! My lawyer threw in a couple of threats for good measure, and after a few weak threat attempts by their attorney, they disappeared. They knew we were right. Game over.

I'm often accused of being too nice, a euphemism for allowing people to take advantage of me. Admittedly, I have a pretty long fuse, wanting to believe the best in people will come through. Crazy, but for a passionate, intense guy, I'm pretty laid back. Over the years, I've had to build self-protection mechanisms against those who mistake niceness with naivete. On the whole, most people I've done business with have been on the up and up, but there have been a few too many charlatans posing as businesspeople, and I've had to adapt and stand my ground against liars, cheats, thieves, and phonies. Regardless, I'd rather be remembered as a nice guy than a bastard, and to this end, I've maintained a friendly, positive, and open-minded character, allowing people a lot of freedom on the various business roads we've traveled together.

Business behavior is made up of so much more than any one characteristic. Experience and judgment. Problem-solving and risk. There's a lot to the things we call creativity and entrepreneurship. Oh yeah, and as I always tell my wife, Kate, I'd rather have my tombstone say I was too nice than that I was a total dick. It doesn't mean I can't be tough. I'm fine with tough. Fine with firing people. Fine with honesty others may not enjoy. I just make more of an effort to find the good in any situation. I learned early on that it would be far too easy to become jaded, hardened, and rude after years of doing business. I've seen it get ugly, but I still say it's best to stay committed to honorable and ethical business practices. Don't allow those who choose to take advantage of others alter your personality for the worse. Stay true to yourself, but develop a bullshit filter that can quickly identify a phony or a slimeball.

Unfortunately for me, reclaiming my product from the engineering company didn't mean I was in the clear with my LandSpeeder business. I still had to decide what to do with all that tooling and where to manufacture the LandSpeeders. I was totally stressed—like, beyond insane. But I had to succeed. Keep moving forward. I searched around, spoke to a variety of shops, and ended up finding an unlikely one-man shop in Bridgeport, Connecticut, that would churn out our frames at the right price, far faster, and with lighter tubing! I redesigned the suspension, cutting out half its weight, and made further changes that improved performance and style while maintaining safety. Believe me, cutting weight and being safe were easy changes given how overbuilt the "pros" had made this thing. Overall, it was crazy, dirty work and a major learning experience on so many levels, from design, engineering, sourcing, and production to assembly, marketing, sales, packaging, shipping, and the seventy-nine other things you take for granted when you're green and launching a new company.

Along the way, this huge undertaking generated no shortage of stories, lessons, heartache, and euphoria. The LandSpeeder was the first production recumbent three-wheeler on the planet, which led to plenty of print and television exposure. Subsequent trade shows proved successful for LandSpeeder, with sales going from three units at our first outing to thirty units at our second show, the New York Bike Show. If you think thirty isn't a lot, try assembling that many. Imagine thirty eight-foot-long vehicles and the space you need for such an adventure. At the rate we were going, just ordering components and the miles of bike chain was a test. Using high school kids as assemblers didn't make life any simpler, but we were making sales, shipping bikes, and putting dollars in the bank. We were headed in the right direction. Or were we? Once again, my creativity itch needed a new scratch.

Having now employed and managed hundreds of people, I realize how shortsighted I'd been when it came to those kids assembling LandSpeeders. For all their desire and commitment, Billy Bob, Michael K., Curt P., and Dave R. unfortunately lacked the appropriate levels of skill, focus, maturity, and consistency for a job that required each bike to work and perform the same. With an endless number of bolts, washers, gears, bearings, springs, cables, chains, levers, and trim details, the LandSpeeder was not an easy product to assemble, even for a bike mechanic. Entrusting it to a bunch of high schoolers was just dumb, but it was a necessity—a budget necessity. Of course, as the saying goes, you get what you pay for. If I had had the brains to pay a little more for mature adults, I would have saved money in the long run, as well as time and distraction. As the boss, you really can't put a price on being distracted from your own, more critical work of managing the entire show. On the other hand, these kids, along with little Tiff McClaskie and Brian Feeley, provided endless comedic moments to punctuate the frustrating times. I'd put their commitment and comradery up against any of the teams

I've built since. Thank you, all of you LandSpeeder workers! We sure had an amazing and memorable adventure.

In relating these stories there is a risk that you might think I knew what I was doing, more or less, right from the start. That I emerged from the womb creative, entrepreneurial, and ready. The reality is I was greener than green, but I was observant, listened to those who had more experience, and learned from them. You might say I absorbed Business 101 knowledge by osmosis. I sought out the advice of those who would serve as early mentors. I have continued to do this throughout my career and, in doing so, have met some truly amazing people, as well as a few who turned out to be truly bizarre.

Of the many highlights and learning experiences associated with the LandSpeeder venture, several stand out:

- *Creating My First Legal Business Entity.* Learning about the various legal entities, tax, and liability ramifications of each, as well as the related legal bills that these adventures create, was a whole new world I didn't want to be part of. This sort of "learning" is a never-ending exercise, as every lawyer you encounter will propose a different approach, regardless of what you've done to date, to fit the changing rules of law. Add to this that regulations and juries increasingly favor the consumer over the business-person, and there are ever-greater demands on you to get your paperwork in order. And don't forget to buy insurance—yet another hassle.
- *Sourcing Parts and Services.* Navigating the highs and lows of locating and then buying parts in bulk, negotiating prices and deliveries, contracting services, and dealing with opportunistic

snakes was tedious at best. It's both exhilarating and daunting when giant boxes arrive loaded with a hundred bike tires or fifty custom-molded fiberglass seats. You get the thrill of production and a sense of *realness*. You also get the packing slips and the invoices and have to pay for these things. Better get busy building and selling!

- *Getting My First Patent.* The LandSpeeder was a hugely detailed patent, and the process proved daunting, given my total lack of experience with patent law and patent lawyers. Thankfully, I later found a good firm, both small and committed, and I use them to this day. My two Davids of Gordon & Jacobson have been a treat to work with, and they understand my nutty ideas and drive to innovate. Now, thirty-five years later, my patent count is a big enough number that I have lost track, but it hardly matters. What matters is the latest project. Always the latest project.

- *Hiring and Training Multiple Employees.* How do you locate, interview, train, and support personnel, especially when you are on a tight budget, want to provide a good work atmosphere, and have loads of other things to do? This is always the biggest expense, so learn fast.

- *Launching a Major Product.* I find that doing PR and convincing the media to look at what I have, especially when it's totally unique and requires a new way of thinking, is both exciting and infuriating at times. It's an ongoing effort that requires real focus. You have to feed the media a stew made of phone calls, mail, visits, and a steady supply of self-produced photos, write-ups, and announcements to compel them to talk about your work.

Expose your product. Learn to talk about it. Generate sales. We did all this before digital, social media and influencers.

+ *Being Interviewed on National TV.* I was asked to bring a LandSpeeder on the CBS Morning News and was interviewed by Bill Curtis, creating a lot of excitement around the bike. They even paid for my assistant and me to stay in an elegant New York City hotel! That felt very Hollywood at a time when any odd bill was tough to swallow.

+ *Shipping Out Real Product.* Every time we loaded one of the giant boxes onto a semitruck, I got such a thrill. It's hard to describe, but it was truly worth all the torture to see each one of my products being sent to a believer. My idea, my baby, our work heading to our *paying* fans. Very satisfying. This emotional high could instantly wipe out stress and frustration.

+ *Being Robbed by An Employee.* I had been out of town, and when I returned, I couldn't put my finger on what looked different. Ah . . . a car was missing—stolen from in front of the shop, then found in New Jersey loaded with my company's parts and products. As an added poke in the eye, when arrested, the ex-employee who stole the car and gear had his parents ask me to help bail him out of jail. Unbelievable.

+ *Realizing I Was Losing My Creative Time to Operational Work.* It was a big shock when I realized I was doing very little creating and a lot of managing, firefighting, and babysitting. This wouldn't end with the LandSpeeder.

+ *Dealing with Employee Car Accidents.* You've already heard the story of young Billy Bob and his trip to pick up the aerodynamic fairing. That's OK, just throw yet another problem on the heap.

- *Learning That Promises Don't Always Count.* From our first manufacturers to my first business lawyer who claimed to know how to sell the business, I was the target of a lot of people who made commitments they wouldn't or couldn't keep. I took two "pro" bike racers with us to the Indy Speedway for the World Speed Championships, expecting our stars to put on a good show with our brand-new consumer product. Well, they did: the girl was painfully slow, all the while making endless excuses, and the big guy got in and promptly vomited all over himself when he realized he had to perform. They were all talk and no go. Embarrassed for my company and my product, I jumped in, dressed in my street clothes, to give us a respectable showing.

Risk and stupidity often go together. The bad and good news is that, over time, the risk went up while the stupidity went down. Once again, I decided to jump ship, starting to remember Tom Feeley's "No M!" The production of bikes had to be one of the crazier undertakings for a beginner in manufacturing, and it was taking a toll. The fun seeped out while the dealings with crummy people increased. Time to sell that venture and see where my ideas would take me.

CHAPTER 6

ADDING FAMILY TO THE MIX

WHILE ALL THE DEMANDING STEPS to building a business and career were testing me daily, I was also busy trying to create a normal family life. I've often wondered, if it takes an unusual character to become an entrepreneur, does it also take an equally unusual character to be married to one? The person who falls for a hypercreative and driven entrepreneur signs on for a potentially long and scary roller coaster ride. While celebrating the highs and enduring the lows, the entrepreneur's mate must learn how to average out these events for any semblance of normalcy if the partnership is to survive.

I once wrote a blog on the myth of work-life balance. Why is this a myth, you might ask? In a word, *balance*. As a serial entrepreneur with a family, what has worked for me and them as a work-life balance is as individual as a fingerprint. Perhaps the reason the issue can be contentious is that everyone has their own opinion on what constitutes balance.

If your definition of *balance* is gauged by the percentage of time at home versus work, you might say, depending on your position, I'm a workaholic destined to fail my family or a lightweight destined for failure in business. What's wrong with conversations on work-life balance, and why it proves elusive, is that we try to define a norm for which no norm exists.

Just as the creative entrepreneur requires a special makeup, so does the mate of the entrepreneur. Theirs must be an innate ability to moderate regular highs and lows while acting as cheerleader, sometime sounding board, and magnet for quirkiness. Their lot in this life comes with the motto, *roll with it.*

I met Kate through her brother, Andy, one of my duck-hunting buddies. A chance invite to a dinner party led to my introduction to Kate, and we hit it off, finding lots of things we liked to do together. Over the years of courtship, Kate spent more and more time at my house in Westport, getting exposed to the variety of people and projects inhabiting Wiener World. Her background was geared toward more stable job styles, so my roller coaster career and ever-changing projects were eye-openers and occasionally quite a challenge for both of us.

For example, I was a terminal car nut, and my most outrageous car purchases happened while I was still single. I wanted to be part of the mid-'80s car business opportunity that emerged for those bold enough to take some big risks, so I started buying and selling Formula One cars. This was as much an adventure of passion as it was a money-making scheme. Locating famously raced cars in Europe taught me new lessons in international business, communications, foreign exchange, purchase contracts, freight, and fear. That was part of the risk and my problem alone. What I never seriously considered was the reaction this new venture might produce from my girlfriend and soon-to-be fiancé.

Reaction is one way to put it. I remember Kate arriving at my home from her teaching job one evening. She happened to look in the garage and saw a stunning white and fluorescent-orange 1979 Alfa-Romeo Formula One car. I knew this because she entered the house at full volume. "What is a Formula One car doing in our garage? What are you doing buying race cars?" I remember my first thought being, *What do you mean* our *garage?* The next, *Are you telling me what I can and can't buy with my own money?* Big questions when you are on the flight path to marriage.

Two more F1 cars followed, with riskier and longer-distance deals making for a true test of character, not to mention future spousal relations. The showstopper came later, during the first days of our honeymoon in Majorca. I was making calls to a buyer in the States who wanted to purchase two of my cars for an exceptional price. Adding to this wonderful little deal was the new Ferrari (wedding gift?) I had ordered to replace the soon-to-be emptiness of my—our—garage. Needless to say, Kate was not pleased that I was conducting business while on a holiday dedicated to her. What can I say? I'm a slow learner. Thankfully, she didn't kill me in those first days of holy matrimony.

To further paint the picture of just how much Kate was *not* a car person, when we first started dating, I figured a romantic walk on the beach would help give things a bit of a shove. At the time, I drove a Ferrari, and I liked that she referred to it as "the red car." But her lack of interest exploded in my face when, after that romantic walk, she jumped back into the car and promptly put her sandy feet up on the dashboard! I was truly biting my tongue. This would be a learning process. But as I said, I liked that she didn't like me for my car.

I'd been in no rush to get hitched and wasn't going to be pressured by my peers, would-be in-laws, or the media. I say *media* because a magazine had decided to include me in their cover story of Connecticut's Ten Most-Wanted Bachelors, which I found both surprising and embarrassing. I guess the other nine guys on the list were honored to be recognized as such, but I found it a bit weird, not to mention hard to explain to the girlfriend who would become my fiancé.

Another memorable test came during our rehearsal dinner, which mixed Kate's Greenwich family and friends with my Westport and Louisiana families. This was sure to cause some fireworks. We'd assembled a large group for a Cajun-themed dinner, complete with one of my uncles, a federal judge and very funny guy, as master of ceremonies. Well, it didn't take long for things to get out of hand. With the bourbon flowing, Kate's family was subjected to no shortage of Cajun duck-hunting jokes replete with backwoods hunting guides, duck blind "theories," discussions of hunting dog anatomy, and a city-slicker hunter or two. As the jokes got raunchier, the room seemed to part like Moses and the Red Sea, with my family and friends laughing hysterically, while Kate's parents and their adult friends cringed. It was palpable. All Kate and I could do was grin and bear it and drink more. Our friends have never let us forget that event!

Thirty-five years later, Kate and I enjoy a marriage and love affair that I think even impresses our kids—not easy to do! Our three boys have tested us and given us endless fun moments in equal parts. My serial entrepreneur gig has also tested us and given us endless fun, though in not-so-equal parts.

Kate dove into the deep end from the start, moving into my house near the beach when we got married. The huge barn on the property was the David Wiener Ventures studio, making my commute very short. Lucky for me, Kate tended a large garden I'd built behind the studio, so I enjoyed a beautiful view of the big back yard and garden from my office in one of the barn lofts. It was all very idyllic, until one day.

I sat working at my desk and noticed something racing down the stone wall that ran the length of the property. Whatever it was had sped along and suddenly dove off the wall and disappeared behind the composter. I watched and waited, but it didn't take me long to figure it out. A big rat had eaten a hole in the back of Kate's plastic compost bin so it could enjoy the food scraps she served up daily. Over the next few days, I paid more attention to the goings on out my office window, watching a regular shuttle run by the intruders. The gauntlet had been thrown down, and I became determined in my quest to eliminate my new distraction. As a competitive shooter, it seemed obvious, albeit completely outrageous, how I'd eliminate the lousy rodents. Forget that we were in the city limits with neighbors all around. This was an emergency. A health hazard. Right?

I come from a family of Louisiana duck hunters, and they gave us two Remington pump guns as a wedding gift—just what Kate wanted! I parked one of the twenty-gauges and a few shells beside my desk. It wasn't long before Mr. Ratty made his move. I opened the loft window and dispatched him with a quick shot. The fact that the carcass flew into my neighbor's yard was of minor consequence (he'd tortured me during the barn renovation). That first shot didn't arouse suspicion, and there were no repercussions: no sirens, no knocks at my door—nothing. Over the next few weeks, I dispatched the clan living under my studio, and we never heard a word from any of the neighbors. Maybe they were too scared, and who knows what Kate was thinking.

The life of a driven and committed entrepreneur takes a significant hit when marriage and kids must become priorities. One day you're powering along, working every hour you can squeeze out of a day (and eating hot dogs), and then suddenly you must fit a new set of responsibilities into your day.

It's a tough pill to swallow when you realize your freedom to focus has been hijacked by your new spouse or infant. Of course, marriage and babies are amazing, transformative events in life, and it's totally possible to be an effective inventor and entrepreneur with a partner and kids. Just be honest with yourself about the impact it will have on your time and energy—of course, there's no knowing ahead of time.

At the same time, many a spouse will remind you over and over that they are the best thing to ever happen to you and that your kids are your greatest creation. Acknowledging both truths will make you a better person. I got absorbed into a lot of family "distraction," but I am glad I did. As much as the time away from work often created stress for me as I worried about hammering through my day's to-do list, the regular break of going home, helping make dinners, feeding, bathing, teaching, and tucking in our three boys created no shortage of fun and important family time. (And I could always resume work when all were finally asleep!)

I will never sound like a Hallmark card and tell you marriage and kids are a walk in the park or all butterflies and unicorns. No—it's been damn difficult a lot of the time, but for me, the good outweighs the pain, and the best part has been watching my kids grow, experience life, and discover their own interests. Remember: the paint isn't dry. Everyone's a beginner at all this family stuff. The results aren't ever totally in, but I'm certain I have done a lot (though not all I could) to help mold, steer, and support my crew. With Kate's amazing efforts, help, humor, and love, we have created a productive and happy family. Like all families, our continued bond has taken hard work all around.

Kate has, no doubt, suffered, having survived almost forty years with a serial entrepreneur—something she grew to understand as we built our life, home, and family together. She would tell you that being the spouse of an entrepreneur is very stressful, given the roller coaster of sporadic paydays, risks, challenges, loans, crazy work hours, and the broad array of personalities that we have dealt with over the years. The fact that all those things energize me to push it even harder has not helped. I've often told her she should have married an accountant. But she didn't. She's hung in there, and we've built a great life together, even if we've been through the meat grinder with a diet of stress and hard work. Surprisingly, some of the hardest moments have actually made us closer and more understanding, even if it didn't feel that way at the time.

Arnold Schwarzenegger stated it very well in his book, *Total Recall: My Unbelievable True Life Story*, while discussing partner problems at home: "My girlfriend of three years was a normal person who wanted normal things and there was nothing normal about me. My drive wasn't normal. My vision of where I wanted to go was not normal. The whole idea of a conventional life was like kryptonite to me."

Kate comes from a place (like most adults) where a weekly paycheck feels a whole lot better than feast and famine. I counter the paycheck complaints with the statement that I have always managed to provide a good, healthy, and fun life for our family. Hell, they call me the Walking Wallet! But I can tell you that this doesn't always cut it. No. An entrepreneur's partner can easily be sent over the edge, courtesy of the stress and uncertainty that creating a new business brings into the bedroom.

Luckily, I have navigated the money game with only a few scars. In most cases, when things were looking their worst, I usually found a way to pull a rabbit out of my hat to bring the sun back over the horizon by securing a major new client, a new investor, or the sale of a business. All of these had a magical way of restoring Earth to spinning on its axis, vanquishing Kate's fears.

Even in the toughest moments, Kate has a beautiful ability to push for peace, love, and friendship. As she says, "Never go to sleep mad," and most of the time, she finds a way to get me laughing—even if it's by kicking me over and over under the sheets until I can't help but laugh. It's the ability to average out the events, listen, call bullshit, and expand life's canvas to include more than work, which makes us tick.

Yet even if I'd known the stress that entrepreneurship puts on a marriage and family, I am not sure I'd have changed a thing. After all, what could I change? Not get married? Become an accountant? Go to work for Kate's father? No! I'm still up to my ears in creativity and entrepreneurship, and my family still has to put up with me.

As if all my regular activities weren't enough to make family life stressful, around 1990, I started pushing the idea of moving away from Westport. Fairfield County was a wonderful place with a nice beach, great boating, and only an hour from Manhattan, but it had become overly affluent, and the newbies had brought too much attitude to town. After a lot of searching for fun spots across the US, in 1991 we bought an incredible piece of land in Aspen—from John Denver! I was thirty-one, and this was only possible because he was selling it off at a bargain-basement price that he was willing to finance for us. Some months into sending checks made out to John Deutschendorf (his real name), I was in Park City for a sports tradeshow and discovered a better spot to raise a family. I signed an offer on a home the next day and quickly moved to sell Aspen, all while trying to keep Kate's head from exploding.

There was even a bit of a marketing lesson in all of this. We put the Aspen land on the market for a very sensible price. It didn't sell. No action. Nothing. I'd been led along by Mark, our Aspen realtor, and we were getting nowhere. Months later, I did the unthinkable: I told Mark to raise the price. He argued with me, but I won. It sold the next day. We just hadn't been thinking big enough. With Aspen sold and Park City in our sights, Kate proposed two years in Park City, but over thirty years later we are still amazed at how well this cross-country adventure has worked out.

They say heaven holds a special place for mothers of three boys. I get it. Unlike Fred McMurray's TV version, our household has been a wild ride, and though our boys are now young men, it's as mystifying as ever. After the arrivals of Weston, Hans, and Enzo, my work and personal life were forced to give way to a new time commitment. I gave up a lot of my activities over the ensuing years and happily focused my home time on various kid activities, education, and sports. From endless school adventures to the equally endless soccer and ski team schedules, we also had our weekly shop time, where I'd hang out with the boys in my home workshop, amid tools, machinery, and materials, hoping something might rub off. In fact, I had visions of raising race-car-driving hunters, fishermen, and ski masters who would make all the fun times even more exciting. I bought an infant-sized race suit before our first child was even conceived. When Weston finally arrived, I was constantly bugging Kate about when he'd be big enough to fit in *the suit*. It took many more months than I'd hoped, but the day finally arrived. Proud dad moment, or as some may have thought, *What's wrong with this guy?*

For all the talk of how my choice of career may have been hard on the family at times, there is another reality: the perks of running my own businesses have allowed me to control my schedule—mostly. I was, and am, home for dinner most nights. I even cooked many of them. This was something I made a priority. Going out for drinks or dinner after work can be a great way to generate new business, but I never prioritized that over my family. Maybe I'm a dopey businessperson for this, but I'm happy about my choice. I think my family is too. And it's not every family that has a full machine shop and sewing studio ready and waiting when Halloween rolls around or the science project needs to have the bar raised, or the Christmas goodies need to get put together with the impossible-to-decipher assembly instructions. Seriously, we still laugh about sending our first two boys to Trick or Treat fully outfitted as Super Pickle and his trusty sidekick, Super Onion! My work has created other family perks, such as adventure vacations, VIP treatment at Formula One races and inside the sacred walls at Ferrari, rides in pace cars, meals at extraordinary places, stays in amazing resorts, backstage fun at concerts, and lots of cool products, clothing, and sports equipment. My family has been on adventures they might otherwise have never experienced, and they've met some amazing people, all because of my work.

Sometimes, these events also mean I've gotten stuck having to make small talk for social or work reasons. Having something to say and being good at small talk are two very different things. I have never been good at small talk—terrible in fact—but I have lots to say and loads to talk about. Just not blabber. Kate, on the other hand, is a master of small talk. She can make conversation with anyone anywhere, and she makes people feel good—comfortable. I am always stunned, impressed—jealous. Kate refers to herself as my secret weapon, knowing she can talk to potential business associates in a way I can't. I just never felt like it was a skill one should aspire to, so I never made an effort. Boy, was I wrong! On the other hand, I can talk with hobos, billionaires, celebrities, CEOs, pro athletes, and famous musicians with comfort and energy as long as the subject matter is interesting.

While I'm on the topic of self-improvement, I should mention I also never bought into networking when I graduated from college. It was another case of me believing it was wrong and only for other people, to push for intros, invites and connections. I was disgusted by a lot of my fellow students who seemed to expect everything to happen for them just because of who they knew or who their family or friends knew. It seemed phony. I believed you had to earn your opportunities. Anyway, I didn't play the game the way others did. I didn't hang out in New York City at the big design events. I didn't mix it up with the hip design people. I didn't *work* it. I'm a slow learner. Oh well, another item for young entrepreneurs to work at. I always wonder how things might have turned out if I'd practiced my craft in New York or San Francisco, where design, creativity, tech, and easy access to investors was, and is, standard fare. I just prioritized a different lifestyle, different kinds of friends, and a different type of family life over maximizing opportunities. And I'm glad I did!

Over the years, our boys pushed the envelope with their own extreme activities, from sports to hobbies to school. It's difficult for teachers to accommodate the kids who color outside the lines or don't always march with the band. Kate and I tried to define boundaries, but they were never designed to restrict thinking outside the lines. In fact, some parents would be shocked at the extreme activities we promoted. We also pushed in some areas that we hoped would encourage family fun down the road.

Kate and I started our boys skiing by carrying them, at age one, in a backpack as we'd fly down Park City Mountain. We then put them on skis at age two, with a ten-foot-long piece of leftover duckboat rope tied around their waists as a leash. To reinforce their love of excitement and speed in the summer, I'd hold them in my lap while racing go-karts at a local spot, making sure we lapped everyone on the track. (Naturally, I had to also reinforce that their dad was the embodiment of *Speed Racer*).

For low-speed fun, we spent many Saturdays in my elaborate workshop. We created all manner of fake guns and swords, always out of raw pine and branded with "TOY" in fat black letters for all the world to see. These guns and swords became the basis of their weekend adventures, with their friends coming over to join in both the shop activities and outdoor battles. Like me, as they got a little older, they wanted to advance and customize their creations, going so far as adding real (and really cheap) scopes on top of their wooden rifles to make them even "cooler."

Over the years, they dove into different activities and then careers of their own. Along the way, my job was to support, guide, sponsor and be very careful not to repeat my father's ways. That was a daily goal of mine and one I continue to consider daily.

As in many families, our boys are all very different yet share a lot of similar behaviors. Weston, as the oldest, blazed a trail for his brothers, and it often did *blaze* as he spurned rules and anything that smelled of boundaries. But his independent spirit—and our constant support— has manifested itself in raw creativity and his passion is movies. Weston creates movies and all the critical elements that make up his projects. Weston's method—writing, designing, directing, and editing—is absolutely impressive to me. While people (and maybe Weston) do not often think about moviemaking as entrepreneurial, Weston's approach to his work is surely entrepreneurial. At thirty-three, he's taking his ideas, applying endless passion, and risking a lot, and that makes his creative, entrepreneurial father very proud.

Hans, our middle guy, took to skiing with such enthusiasm that he pushed me to be a better skier as we'd fly down ski runs, me ten feet behind, hanging onto that old rope as he'd yell, "Faster, faster!" The whole time I'd be thinking, *What if he falls at that speed? I'd have to jump over him because there's no way I'd be able to stop in time.* Well, Hans turned out to be the instigator who, when he was about eight years old, talked his brothers into joining him on our pitched roof, to snowboard off into the darkness. I know this only because I spotted them one night when I returned from work. As I drove up our driveway, I noticed three little animals on our roof. Sorry, not animals—three little maniacs. On the peak of the roof! I promptly parked my car in the garage, went inside, and poured a stiff drink. Hans became a pro freeride skier, launching himself off things that most parents viewed as a clear indicator of bad parenting. I was so proud!

Hans has taken his lack of fear in various directions, pursuing modeling, acting, real estate—and still more extreme ski competitions. You can't choose many tougher professions to break into, but Hans has shown courage, applying that leap-off-tall-buildings fearlessness as he forges his own path.

Our youngest, Enzo, benefited from watching his two older brothers explore way too many outrageous activities, and from this he has emerged as the mature one. His brothers turn to him for advice, and it's amusing to witness this evolution. Our boys are growing together, even after squabbles, fights, blood, and even a broken leg (one boy running the other over "by accident" with his bike). Enzo's passions mix elite soccer and economics, and it shows as he brings a competitor's no-lose attitude to his work in venture capital. He's been steeped in the entrepreneurial life, growing up in our house and my offices, and it would take just a nudge to push him into a start-up or new venture of his own. This could happen at any time. All it will take is the right idea and his existing passion.

The boys may be older now, but they haven't eased up on me. They were never easy on me. Their comments and critiques, along with Kate's, were, and are, a test. So, how do you deal with family when they get all up in your business? And I do mean *business*. Unless you are fully debriefing your family about your business on a daily basis, they generally have little knowledge of the myriad activities, responsibilities, schedules, and problems that are a daily grinder.

It's hard to regularly share what it's like to work twelve to eighteen hours a day; be responsible for multiple projects, people, and deadlines that impact your customers (and their customers); and make decisions that will have an impact weeks, months, and years into the future—decisions that will impact the creative entrepreneur, the family, the employees, and beyond.

It's also hard for family to understand that coming home at the end of a long day and instantly shifting into home mode isn't so instantaneous. There's always another work-related idea, an email, a call—something that could make *the difference*. They just know they want Dad, David, home. Whatever work came before that moment is unknown and irrelevant.

So how do you manage? What do you bring home and what do you leave at the office? I've found that sharing some details of my day or my work has always been a double-edged sword. On one side, my wife and kids may be dying to know what the latest news is, but there's always the risk of them knowing just enough to be dangerous, mostly to me. For example, if you mention something about trouble with an employee or frustration with a vendor, weeks later, you may get hit over the head with it, along with some Monday-morning quarterbacking, as your wife or kids spout some completely misguided "advice."

While you might share information about your latest project, underperforming employee, newest customer, problems with manufacturing, or whatever else you need to purge, realize your family is processing these data points in a different way than you may have intended to communicate them. You are sharing these tidbits because you want to inform them, or more likely, you just need to get some things off your chest. But when they hear your news, they may feel a need to assist, offer advice, or play an active role in your business. Often it's hard for them to have a full understanding of the situation, but they'll respond regardless because it's human nature. There's a reason people talk about unsolicited advice.

"You need to get rid of so-and-so."

"You shouldn't have done so-and-so."

"You should've charged more."

"That employee is useless."

All these and so many more pieces of expert commentary make me never want to share anything about my work. Imagine if NFL commentators had never actually played the game. You get the idea.

In the end, most family and friends will offer you advice because they genuinely care about you and want to help find solutions. Your family in particular doesn't want to see you stressed, angry, or frustrated. They want to help, jump into the fray, and offer solutions, even if they are misguided. Try to remember their good intentions as your blood pressure rises.

I am not suggesting I'm closed to advice or criticism. Quite the opposite is true, but I want advice and critique from people who have expertise and have all the facts. I also want to state the obvious: lots of professionals go through the exact same thing, but the difference is most are not entrepreneurs. They have the luxury of being able to hand off issues, take credit, or blame their boss, all while collecting a regular paycheck.

On the other hand, my family sure does love it on success day, and there's nothing more satisfying for me than treating them to some spoiling: gifts, a trip, a good meal out, whatever. Beyond creating my next product or venture, spoiling my family is my greatest joy. It truly doesn't matter if it's cooking them a meal, driving them at one hundred miles per hour, teaching them to shoot shotguns, covering a rent check, or buying them a bauble. They may not even notice (or remember) it much of the time, but I know, and that is what gives me pleasure.

CHAPTER 7

NO FOCUS

MY PROBLEM HAS ALWAYS BEEN FOCUS. I've always been excited by a lot of things at once, which isn't focus at all. It's very exciting—and great for my creativity—but it's not the best approach for growing a business. Regardless, it's what I've mostly done. In the early days, I was hunting for ways to be creative *and* earn money. Going from cars to furniture to fashion and beyond made for an interesting life and career. Still does. There's a lesson in this somewhere.

I never really thought I'd get involved with fashion, even though I'd had several ideas about how to improve some of the sports clothing I'd owned. As a kid growing up skiing, ski racing, and teaching skiing, I always thought the available ski fashions were lacking, some in performance, others in style. I had ideas, lots of them, and at the beginning of my career, I made time at night to work on a nonwork project.

I borrowed a sewing machine and parked it in my bedroom. At night, after work, I'd turn the clothing in my closet inside-out and analyze the construction methods, applying engineering eyes to what others would call sewing. I bought an assortment of fabrics, exhausting the local homemakers' store before scouring interior design shops in search of unique materials that would be all the more unusual when applied to clothing. These couch and curtain fabrics weren't created with Olympic ski racing in mind, but no matter—I figured I could spray them with waterproofing later.

So there I was, in my little rented house, squeezed between the TV and the end of my bed, experimenting. I tried making different types of seams, patches, pleats, and combinations of materials (fabric, Mylar, rubber, etc.), creating a variety of both odd and cool samples that I could test-drive and see if my ideas were worth pursuing. After a few months of experiments, I'd filled a big duffle with samples and figured it was time. I'd expose my ideas to someone in the fashion world and take a licking while learning what my next step should be: continue or quit.

Since my focus was skiwear, I made a few calls and arranged to show my stuff to someone at the then-largest and most popular skiwear brand in America, CB Sports, whose logo has been described in the media as "the lift-line equivalent of the Lacoste alligator." I knew absolutely nothing about fashion, the skiwear business, or the mass production of clothing. I didn't know sewing terminology or the sources for "real" fabrics. Hell, I didn't even know what the proper materials should be beyond reading a few trademarked names off hangtags at ski shops. I did know C. B. Vaughn was a skiing legend and a huge success, making him the right person to work with.

I drove four hours to a meeting at CB Sports, where I explained that I was not a fashion designer and that I'd created some samples to see where it might lead, and could they please provide some guidance.

After two review sessions, I was asked to wait in the lobby while C. B. and Susan, his number two, conferred. I was thinking, *OK, this is bad. He hates it, and he's going to tell Susan to let me down gently.*

After what felt like forever, I was asked to return to the conference room. CB announced that they wanted me to design their next two lines, to which, I surely must've responded, "What?"

"Our next two lines. Can you do it?"

"Of course I can," I stuttered.

I left with a contract to design fashion. Me. Fashion. Seriously? The four-hour ride home was a tape loop that played in my brain: "What's a line? What's a line? What's a line? What's a line?" I knew what the word meant, but I had zero idea what *they* believed it meant and what I was supposed to deliver. These were to be two brand-new lines—not updates of their existing lines—but beyond that, they left it to me. They didn't provide outlines, lists, requirements—nothing. I had given them enough new ideas that they wanted to launch completely new lines, while their time-honored pieces were relegated to the backseat. I was getting the dream shot. My ideas. My designs. My views on how skiwear should perform. My aesthetic as applied to ski fashion. In short, I could design whatever I wanted. What had I bitten off this time? This would become a recurring theme and emotional minefield: the absolute thrill of validation and financial success muted by the total fear of possibly delivering a bomb.

Another thought rolled around in my head: how would their in-house designers react to C. B. bringing in an outsider? Thankfully, my confidence level, having just been dramatically boosted, allowed me not to dwell on that one.

I survived the drive home. I followed up the next week, getting more details out of them, along with a nice check. Time to get to work.

Over the next few months, I made countless sketches and then refined them into proper drawings—proper to me that is, since I had no idea what was expected. And as with every other project I'd ever done, especially the ones where I thought my entire career hinged on the work, I went overboard. Way overboard! I invented and designed the two lines, including the names, logos, branding, fabric patterns, hardware, patches, and stitching details. One was full-race Olympic-level skiwear and training gear, and the other, Advanced Performance System (APS), was an all-round, high-end skiwear collection. I designed "engineered" clothing, accessories, bags, and more.

I brought a lot of ideas, creativity, new approaches, and real-world user expertise to bear as I finished the project. What I didn't bring to bear was any form of sanity. I went crazy. I created so many pieces of clothing and gear that they wouldn't need me to do a second season for probably eight seasons! Another bit of inexperience that I would repeat on future projects simply out of passion and excitement (and a need to wow C. B. and company). This exuberance is the entrepreneurial spirit unleashed. Unlike many designers or consultants who come in, deliver the product, and leave with a check, I felt as much passion to launch the products I'd created for CB Sports as I did with any of my own product launches. The pay was good—great—especially for a first-time fashion designer, but the money, while always needed to fuel the next experiment, was secondary. I was thrilled to be doing this job, just like a Formula One driver who gets paid a lot of money but would gladly do it for free, just to be in the game.

The CB team was thrilled, much to my relief. They went wild with all the drawings, working to produce what I had created. As C. B. said in a letter to me on July 25, 1988, "We are all excited about the work that you did on the Advanced Performance System, and we hope this is the beginning of what will be a long and rewarding relationship for all of us. Both Susan and I feel strongly about trying to come up with a commitment to each other that would enable you to have CB Sports as your only clothing client."

Unbelievable. All this thanks to a bagful of samples I made in my bedroom! After the skiwear project, CB Sports contracted me to design an entire collection of retail fixtures, signage, and point-of-purchase displays to make the CB Sports skiwear I'd designed stand out in typically overcrowded ski shops.

Again, I went off the deep end. I designed the display fixtures I imagined would create a more exciting shopping experience. I didn't know what I was doing, but as my mother always said, I knew what I liked, and I was creating the kind of stuff I'd like to see in the ski shop of my dreams. I knew how to dream big, especially about skiing. I'd worked in two ski shops during my high school years: Sport Mart in Westport and the famous Hickory and Tweed in Armonk, New York—the creation of Jimmy Ross, one of the most charismatic personalities from the world of skiing at that time. I'd done everything from mounting bindings to selling equipment to exterior painting—all of it a thrill for a ski-mad kid. And now I was going to leave my mark on the world of skiing, or so I believed.

This project and my imagination allowed me to put my furniture and manufacturing experience to work as I invented unique waterfall racks, mountaintop-shaped full-length mirrors, icicle overhead lighting, and life-size cut-outs of C. B. himself, complete with downhill skis and other high-visibility fixtures.

In the end, the APS collection became CB Sports' bestselling line, worldwide. Of course, with all I had created, I was now a fashion designer with nothing to do. I decided there was another area of fashion interest that would combine my love of performance and style with activities dear to my heart. I used the experience from my life of fishing and hunting and created a collection of clothing and accessories geared to European bird shooting and saltwater fly fishing. I named the line Pheasant Hill and eventually sold it to Beymen, a luxury fashion conglomerate in Istanbul.

I was about thirty when I was approached by Columbia Sportswear to create the brand for a line of fly fishing clothing. Naturally, I said yes. I was a totally committed saltwater fly fisherman, and they knew it. My company created a name and logo that would become icons of the fishing and outdoor clothing industry. It didn't take long before they realized we had a lot more capability than just branding and graphics. Once Columbia learned of my years of experience with high-performance fashion design for skiing, hunting, and fishing, they asked me to rework their clothing designs. By the time I was done, I'd reinvented their fishing clothing and created a line that I was sure would be a hit. Unfortunately, some of the top salespeople at Columbia were not so sure.

Columbia had presented my creations, which I had branded Performance Fishing Gear (PFG), to their sales team so they could give their two cents. The report I got back was "This line will never sell. There isn't a market for fly fishing clothing." They knew a few companies had tried to sell fishing clothes but hadn't made much of an impact. I didn't know Columbia's sales guys, but I wasn't going to let my Columbia point person, Bart, and the others fold. I started a fight. I pushed and pushed and told the key people why this product line made sense. It wasn't easy, and it wasn't fast. I had to repeat myself over and over, all by phone, from three thousand miles away!

Finally, after a lot of back-and-forth, Columbia's matriarch (Ma Gert) and her boys decided to take a risk. Smart move! For thirty years, PFG clothing has been the bestselling product line in the fishing industry, becoming hugely popular with not just fishermen but active people and travelers around the globe. You can see my distinctive triangular PFG logo everywhere. Lightweight, comfortable, and easy to clean on the go, the PFG line is the standard by which sportsmen and world travelers judge all other clothing. In fact, this concept of sportsmen-oriented clothing has spawned a wide variety of companies targeting fishing, hunting, hiking, mountaineering, camping, and more. If you go to any of the giant fishing and sporting goods retailers like Bass Pro Shop, Cabela's, West Marine, and Dick's Sporting Goods, you will see more floor space devoted to PFG than almost any other product.

As Bart wrote in a testimonial a short time later, "David is in touch with the sports industry and as a result brings a greater design sensitivity to each and every project. He produces innovative, fresh creative solutions that get the job done!" So much for the sales experts. Were any of them even fly fishing guys?

In another odd career moment, around 1990, I received a call from a company saying they'd heard about our work and wanted to have DWV create the logo for their new aircraft company. I was happy to consider any outside project as long as it fit my performance, aesthetic, and excitement requirements. In other words, anything we took on had to be unique, timeless, devoid of trendiness, and able to perform at the highest level for the given application. We set a meeting, and they came to the DWV studio. I gave my usual intro, describing all the things we were involved in. They then explained their logo need and the fact that they were creating an innovative ground-effects aircraft designed to take off and land in water. They had bold visions of commercial and recreational sales; owners would not need a pilot's license for this type of aircraft since a motion-generated cushion of air would keep the plane aloft flying fifteen feet or so above the water while in forward flight. After an hour of discussion and a more detailed explanation of the kinds of projects my team had worked on, their CEO, Bill Russell, stopped me and said, "Forget the logo. I want you to design the aircraft." I shook his hand and said, "Sure, we can do that!" Sure . . .

I'd studied aerodynamics. I'd designed cars. I could do this. We could do this! Couldn't we? I'd recently invested in a truly amazing Silicon Graphics 3D computer modeling system, and this aircraft project would justify the entire investment. We could do this! Our job would be to work with the other engineers on the project, including well-known aeronautics and yacht design experts, and then shape the craft to combine high performance and sleek styling.

As the project moved forward, the design turned into a full-scale prototype to be used for test flights, demonstrations, and promotion. It was exciting to accompany the team up to Rhode Island where the craft was being fabricated. Walking on the nose of the craft and looking at all the details, curves, and fillets was a powerful experience. Seeing your ideas and designs turned into reality is always exciting. To see it on this scale was off the charts.

My design would eventually end up on the cover of *Popular Science*, which was beyond our wildest (promotional) dreams. This news pushed me to advance my skills in what would later be generically considered photoshopping. To elevate our computer-generated, 3D-rendered image of the craft, I shot photos to place two people inside the cockpit and create a backdrop of Long Island Sound, complete with boats, birds, and buoys. This was a big moment for the Flarecraft execs, as their plane and name would be getting huge exposure on the cover and a feature article inside. Unfortunately, after all the careful manipulation to create a convincing image of the Flarecraft in flight, the legal team at *Popular Science* balked at the idea that readers might sue if they tried to order a Flarecraft only to be told the image was fake. I had to start all over and create a more computer-generated-looking image that finally made the cover. The bonus round to all of this: the Alias 3D software people loved us when we relayed the story that the craft looked "too real" according to the people at *Popular Science*, dream words to any 3D software company. They were so excited they created an entire ad campaign around our Flarecraft design. The amusing point to me is that while our 3D work was cutting edge at the time, viewing it today, decades later, it looks totally amateurish. That's progress!

Bill wrote a statement at some point after all this took place: "I have worked with David over many years, on very difficult design issues with the Flarecraft. David is not only a pleasure to work with, but the most talented designer I have ever hired." Well, I guess he wasn't kidding because some years later, Bill approached me to design a completely new Flarecraft that used emerging technology and allowed me to apply my additional years of design, engineering, and production experience to create a truly realistic head-turning 3D modeled aircraft.

In 1997, I was as unfocused as ever. While we were creating product ideas and developing an audio speaker business, my endless love of auto racing and the need for new ventures led to a variety of image and sponsorship business ideas. It started with motorsports, then moved to yacht racing, which led to other high-profile and exciting opportunities that were hard for me to resist. Our image consulting work expanded with a variety of interesting and important clients, including the then-new Utah Winter Sports Park, site of the 2002 Winter Olympics bobsled, luge, skeleton, and Nordic ski jumping events. Once again, we were asked to create a logo and brand for them, and once again, everyone was happy with the result. The next project would eclipse this.

The US Ski Association (USSA, the governing body for the US Ski Team and US Snowboard Team) was doing a national search for an image and branding agency to give them a makeover. They were looking at some of the top agencies in the United States, and thankfully, someone told them to look at David Wiener Ventures. After going through a significant proposal process, explaining my theories, and how we would go about their project, we were awarded the account and got to work researching their current activities, assets, and shortcomings, along with developing concepts for their new image.

As a kid, I had been obsessed with skiing, and to all of us young ski racers in training, the US Ski Team logo was an icon of our dreams. Only a select few would ever get to wear it, but dreaming was free. Fast-forward and suddenly I was in charge of creating a new icon. Once again, my personal excitement and respect for the brand, image, and what it represented in the world had me shifting into hyper-mode. I wanted this to be great. If done well, it would last a long time, and that meant it had to be timeless.

While I coordinated and led a lot of meetings and assorted personalities at USSA, I was also working on ideas to make over that legendary Ski Team logo. Although we were tasked with revamping USSA's entire image, the logo would be the key element of the entire project and the basis on which we would be judged. Along the way, I had some great battles with one of their top generals who had his own—and I'd say antiquated—ideas. Thankfully, I wasn't an employee, and the worst I'd risk was him arguing with me in front of his team. I was confident in my approach and ideas and was able to navigate this one-man storm unscathed.

In the end, we created new logos for the US Ski Team, the US Snowboard Team, and the United States Ski Association, along with a long list of collateral, graphics, branding guidelines, medals, clothing, posters, decals, and more. Most satisfying was the dramatic unveiling and overwhelming reaction to their most valuable marque and asset, the US Ski Team logo, which created twenty-plus years of brand and commercial success. In the words of Tom Kelly, USSA's VP of marketing, "We conducted a national agency search to manage the project, selecting David Wiener Ventures. DWV did an extraordinary job creating a design that positions the new mark to be one of the most exciting in Olympic sport. USSA is proud of its image and its brands have risen in value since initiating its image makeover. David Wiener Ventures made the difference!"

Another out-of-nowhere image project we did was for Deer Valley Ski Resort, regularly voted the best in many categories. Their official vacation and lodging group manages a variety of high-end hotels and luxury condominiums, and they wanted DWV to analyze the image, aesthetics, and operation of these elegant properties and then outline a plan to improve each facility and the company overall. A perk of this project was taking my family to each location to enjoy the luxury, food, drink, comfort, and skiing each had to offer. My sons enjoyed this "work" the most, given the monstrous suites, countless recreational opportunities, and "all the free stuff." Not so bad having a creative entrepreneur for a dad after all.

Most of the consulting projects I've done have come out of left field. Chip Ganassi Racing was no different when they approached me to create the image of their new IndyCar team. They were already a famous championship team with Michael Andretti and Target sponsorship, but as any self-respecting racing impresario knows, expansion is the key to creating wealth, so Chip was going to field a second team with sponsorship from the South American Hollywood cigarettes brand. Exciting as it was for me, the bonus round was that they had signed a former Formula One driver and protégé of Ayrton Senna as their new pilot. I was going to get to design the cars, uniforms, team equipment, and merchandise, and I was going to get to hang out with Mauricio Guggelmin and others tied to the new team. Another dream project!

I thought I was going to have total freedom to design the car and cement myself in the pantheon of the outrageous. Then the Hollywood machine got in my way. I created several high-visibility designs that would make the new Ganassi team stand out from all others on the grid. I sent them to Hollywood in Brazil so they could choose, and what do you know, committees always choose the most conservative of the lot. I was so pissed. I felt I knew what would work, but oh well. An Indy car is a whole lot better than no Indy car, so I went to work preparing the artwork for the paint and decal suppliers. Then I went a little farther. I needed to exercise my creativity a bit more, so I created some extra details and sent the files to the decal maker. The first testing days were only days away. The car had been painted per my drawings, and I was supposed to be at the track to supervise the application of the decal art to the car. I was pretty excited. My first real race car! David Wiener Ventures' first real race car!

I arrived and found a box full of huge decals—and my "extras." I'd created aero vortex stripes to enhance the overall design, and I couldn't wait to see the completed car in real life. In the end, it looked great, and everyone loved it. I'd slid by with a few unauthorized elements, and as a bonus round, I got to see my work turned into a mass-produced, miniature, collectible model car. That was a surprise. For a car-racing fanatic, this was a wonderful tribute, or so I told myself. Who says model cars are for kids?

The Ganassi Racing project launched my company's efforts to do more race team design. I figured we had done work for one of the top teams, so we ought to be able to do it for a whole bunch of others. "Stand out from the crowd" was my theme. After all, if you're going to spend all that money for visibility and attention, you owe it to yourself to do it right.

Expanding our sports image program, I tapped my experience with yacht racing, a perfect complement to our new motorsports business. Designing racing yachts would give me an even bigger canvas to play with, and our first yachting customer gave us free rein to design the livery for his brand-new Mumm 36 boat, *Fast Tango*, and team gear, which led to an exciting program and fun times going down to Key West Race Week to install the team livery, deliver the clothing, and shoot photos of the whole thing.

I didn't realize just how hard designing for the Mumm yacht racing series could be. Key West. Endless drinking. Little sleep. Trying to be professional. My first task was applying thirty-foot-long decals to the boat while balancing in a dinghy in between two large racing yachts. No room to maneuver, I was alone in my task, and the clock was ticking, as usual.

The culmination of this project was shooting photos out on the ocean from a thirteen-foot Boston Whaler, the only boat I could find. The owner was young and scared. It took me a while to grind him down and build up his courage. It also took some cash. I think he was intimidated at the thought of piloting his small craft in those ocean swells, but I wasn't going to give up (remember my hydroplane?), and I think he knew it. I finally got him to agree to take me out to the racecourse so I could document the *Fast Tango* and crew. We lived! A week later, the racing boat's owner, Tim Prophit, called me up and gushed that *Fast Tango* was the most photographed boat at the entire Key West Race Week. Then it was in all the sailing magazines. What can I say, that was the goal: stand out from the crowd—even on the water!

With all these projects, people, and industries, a studio full of ideas, and a house full of samples, it was time to go big. Finally. Just maybe, if I focused, I could create that next big thing.

CHAPTER 8
FOCUS

TURNS OUT MY MILLION-DOLLAR IDEA was almost twenty years in the making. For no obvious reason, around 1982 I got a crazy idea for an audio speaker system born of a wild aesthetic inspiration: a piece of industrial vent hose hanging in a store window on Canal Street in New York City. I was freshly installed in my first rented house, with little furniture and wild ideas about decorating the place. I bought a twenty-foot-long piece of twelve-inch-diameter hose, laid it on the floor at home, and stared at my new silver-gray accordion snake, wondering how best to utilize this obviously cool piece of high-tech hardware. "High Tech" was big in the early '80s, the idea being that industrial materials and hardware could be used to create consumer-oriented home furnishings. I spent weeks thinking about that snake in the middle of my living room. Finally, it hit me: create a gigantic tubular speaker to make music even cooler. Why not?

I bought some basic speaker parts: two woofers, two tweeters, and two crossover circuits, and I devised a method of mounting this gear inside each end of my twenty-foot monster. It sounded OK and got better—maybe—when I hung it from the ceiling, or it might have been that I'd turned it way up. Everything sounds better loud. My friends thought it was cool, so I made a few copies and sold them. Along the way, the audio store sales guys I consulted for advice told me I was crazy, and then they'd sell me some more stuff.

I made tweaks to my design, but other projects took priority, and my focus was diverted on a regular basis. I used the speaker prototypes at home, but it wasn't until some nine years later that I made a major change to the design. I realized that despite my enthusiasm for big and wild, a twenty-foot speaker hose was not something most people would want in their homes. I miniaturized. I went down to four feet long and eight inches in diameter—positively tiny! I also made the speakers sound better by mounting the tweeters on adjustable arms so they could be aimed at the listener, regardless of which way the hose pointed. (It's interesting to note that years later, all the major home speaker manufacturers would be making adjustable tweeters for this exact purpose.)

The design and engineering development were intriguing, but still, I wasn't sure I'd ever get to something truly salable. As usual, I parked it for a spell as more pressing work got in the way, not to mention a move from Connecticut to Utah.

It was 1994. I was happily settled in Park City with a new staff of five and the usual assortment of projects when I made an announcement to my team: we were working on too many things. I was finally maturing and realizing it was time for a big success. I needed it to convince myself that all the work to date and all the struggles had been worth it. I also wanted a big financial success. I needed it. We were scattered. Our brains were scattered. I wanted to focus. Choose one thing and make it amazing.

I asked for input on which of our projects they each thought made the most sense. Which had the best chance for commercial success? Was it our motorsports image consulting service, fashion line development, product consulting, or something new? In the end, as boss, I knew I held the one vote. I also knew what I wanted to do: the speaker that I had kind of obviously dubbed SoundTube. After a lot of debate, I pulled rank and made it clear we would put all our projects on indefinite hold and focus on SoundTube. Total commitment. Total focus! This would be a major effort to produce a product we could sell in quantity. It was a bet-the-farm moment, and I was doing it of my own choice. I wasn't being forced. No one was advising me to do this. I had no way to know where it might lead. What I did know, from personal experience, was that if I didn't focus my energy and creativity, I might never achieve my real goals.

In 1995, DWV spun off a new company, SoundTube Entertainment, to provide the best sound solution for commercial venues. We chose commercial over consumer figuring pro customers would be more demanding. We'd learn faster in a fire. I spent weeks developing a business plan and camping out in the Park City library to escape the phones and distractions at the office. For perspective, our office at that time was one large room overlooking Main Street with five people crammed together, phones ringing, music blaring, and conversations unending.

At the same time, I got serious about creating a viable speaker product, filling my home garage with all kinds of prototypes. One of my employees, Tom Gorton, was a graphic artist, bass player, and music lover. He became my default shop assistant. We would screw parts together and drag them upstairs to the living room, where we'd connect some wires and play Zeppelin at full blast to see how we were doing. Not very scientific, but listening tests sure were fun.

And occasionally weird.

Tom and I had put in a long Saturday one weekend when my family was out of town. After our shop marathon and subsequent rock-fest audio test, we decided to take a break and have a beer on my deck, music blaring. Beers led to martinis. This being Park City, a resort ski town, we had daily hot air balloons giving tourists rides high in the sky. In our rocking chairs, martinis flowing, we thought it would be cool to actually see the people in the balloons. I grabbed some big military-style binoculars left over from my Pheasant Hill hunting clothing photo shoots, and we scanned our target. Not powerful enough.

But I got an idea.

I had a brand-new black hunting rifle that looked more SWAT than hunter. I sat in one rocker looking through the powerful scope while Tom, in his rocker, stared through the big binoculars at the same target. All was fine until a hiker, coming off the mountain trail, walked past the deck, looked over, and saw two guys surrounded by beer bottles and martini glasses, pointing a sniper rifle and binoculars at innocent tourists in a hot air balloon. Needless to say, he assumed the worst, let out a scream, and ran. That's when Tom and I gathered up all the mess and raced back to the garage.

Given my lack of acoustic engineering expertise, I enlisted some outside help for the audio engineering element, as we toiled away, cut tubing and experimented with speakers, sound reflectors and other odd concepts. I had lots of unique ideas but no clue how to create a well-balanced sonic device. What parts, performance parameters, and testing procedures did we need? I knew what I didn't know, and I wasn't afraid to admit it. So I hired a speaker consultant, which was an adventure in itself, as this guy, and most that followed, would never admit that there was anything they didn't know! Luckily, I was able to keep him bridled, and the results eventually materialized. After countless experiments, we came up with an innovative product, but as always seemed to be the case, this one would require manufacturing methods that were new to me.

Over the following months, we built a series of samples that we could demonstrate, install for promotional photography, and use to practice sales. Taking a chance, I introduced myself to the two women in charge of the World Cup ski races that took place every November at Park City. Next thing I knew, we were building our first production speakers for the celebrated America's Opening, the first stop on the alpine ski racing World Cup circuit. The stress was insane, and I surely lost some of my lifespan during that time. But somehow we pulled it off, hanging giant speakers all around the race arena.

Focusing on the commercial audio market, we needed a couple of years to finally break through, convincing professional sound engineers and installers, along with retail and restaurant chains, that our odd, tubular speakers with their omnidirectional dispersion system actually worked. It wasn't until we secured all of the Old Navy stores, beating out Bose and JBL, that we got any respect, but then we were on our way. Next, we won the Gap account, refitting all their stores, followed by many others. Over the following years, Starbucks, Whole Foods, Zuppa's, and a long list of international retail stores, restaurants, airports, theme parks, and sports venues converted to SoundTube speakers—indoors and out.

Of course, along the way to growing what would become one of the leading brands in commercial audio speakers, we suffered countless problems, from manufacturing to vendors to shipping to cash flow. It was a constant struggle, punctuated with a lot of exciting moments and interesting people. There are too many stories to recount, so I'll limit myself to just a small sampling.

In developing the unusual first SoundTube speakers, I had to learn about molding plastic. This led me to vacuum molding. I ended up in Elkhart, Indiana, the Mecca for vacuum molding thanks to the motorhome industry. Unfortunately, the molder I was pointed to, possibly because of our tight budget, turned out to be one of those too good to be true situations. I kept forgetting my thing about *you get what you pay for.* The short version of the Indiana story is that the parts started to arrive after many weeks, and I started signing big checks—but not in that order. As speakers started coming together, we discovered great variations in the seven different plastic parts that went into each SoundTube. This made production very slow and resulted in a parts rejection rate of about 40 percent, not a workable path to profitability. Many frustrating calls later, I decided it was a lost cause. I hunted for a new molder. To my great relief, I worked out a deal with a company in Salt Lake City, right down the road from Park City, meaning I could keep an eye on them. More expensive, but you get what you pay for!

This change meant I had to tell Indiana I was leaving, and I wanted my molds. "Not so fast, Henry Ford. To get your molds, you need to pay off your account." They didn't want to accept responsibility for all the returned parts, and they held my molds hostage. Needless to say, I had to get the molds so we could produce product. I paid the piper and waited. When the molds arrived at our new Salt Lake City vendor, I received word that the molds were useless junk. Time to start over, spend more money, waste time, delay production, get an ulcer, and use creative genius to plot revenge.

To you, reading this may sound like a frustrating setback, but at the time, it felt like a death blow. One big check followed another big check. More months to wait for new molds. The business needed to be selling, not waiting.

Business Lesson #53: *signed* agreements need to spell out part quality, performance standards, quality-control methods, and tooling (molds in this case) quality, durability, and maintenance, along with ownership details. I learned the hard way.

Working from our one-room Main Street office gave the team a real sense of unity, whether we were listening to each other's phone sales techniques or pouring martinis, beers, and Jägermeister shots.

Building early-production SoundTubes in my home garage gave the impression we were doing something truly unique, as if we were pioneers. It felt like a mixture of mass production and school. To us, it felt like an assembly line.

Launching SoundTube came with much more than just a load of personal risk—both financial and mental. It also meant that at some point we'd actually have to launch our product, and it would have to fly or crash. That's how black and white it felt to me. The first public installation of these highly unusual speakers was scheduled for America's Opening. We'd convinced Park City Ski Resort to use the speakers to create a sonic and visual corridor from the parking lot up to the finish area of the racecourse. The who's who of the international ski world would be there, along with international press and TV crews. It would be outdoors, winter, possibly snowing, and everything had to work, and working meant hanging the SoundTubes from cables strung high up across chairlift towers and phone poles. This wasn't going to be easy. In fact, it was probably the toughest install we could imagine, and it would be our maiden voyage. We were being paid—that was amazing under the circumstances—and this put even more pressure on us for the speakers to perform.

Already an incredibly tough balancing act—work and family—it's a lot tougher when your product launch to the world is taking place on Thanksgiving in Utah and you are scheduled to take your family back to Connecticut for the Thanksgiving holiday.

Just getting the multiple SoundTubes built and working was hard enough. Time and construction details were working against us to get the products assembled and installed on schedule. We were pulling all-nighters, and everyone was ragged. Our production facility at the time was my garage, and that meant my family was one floor up, wondering what, and how, we were doing and whether we'd achieve our goal.

As dawn broke on the Wednesday before the holiday, I was spent, exhausted at a level I'd never known. I was on the verge of a breakdown of some sort, and I didn't know what to do. Stay home and toil more or keep my commitment to my wife, kids, and extended family?

Was this worth it, torturing myself? And it was torture. Self-torture. I wanted success. I wanted to prove I could do what I set out to do. I also didn't relish the idea of my family being totally let down by my priorities. Truly one of the hardest moments I'd ever experienced to that point. I wanted to cry. I never cry, but I felt like I had no control.

After the predawn hours of pondering the nightmare, I made some calls and made my decision—the biggest moment of delegating in my then-short career. I told my work crew that I was putting the entire event in their hands and that I was traveling to Connecticut to spend Thanksgiving with my family. It was somehow both freeing and incredibly stressful, but I did it. I got on the plane. Kate and the kids had no idea just how much it was eating me alive. They were lucky in that they could just mindlessly move forward, quickly dismissing my stress as soon as I announced my decision.

This was a turning point of sorts. I'd learned to let go (a little). Learned to delegate. Learned that things I was convinced only I could manage were quite possibly doable by others. The hard part in admitting this during Thanksgiving was that we were still in the early days of mobile phones, so checking in with the team as they toiled in the snow doing the installation was tough. I was stuck in Connecticut, staring at family and food, hotel rooms, and three active little kids while constantly wondering what was happening at the World Cup. As I often respond to complainers, "no one died," and I guess this could be applied to the SoundTube World Cup coming-out party. My team made it work, and I survived, but the overall stress had begun to drill a hole in me. The World Cup was a success, but SoundTube was still in its infancy.

Post–World Cup, we got down to making product and convincing people to buy. The excitement of shipping our first order was palpable. I remember taking photos as two of our team ran a large box down Main Street to catch the UPS truck passing our office. Soon after, we'd get our own UPS account, and the big brown truck would come to my house (the shop) around five each day. Our UPS driver, Chad, became a loyal friend to SoundTube as he helped us with last-minute box taping so we could get shipments out. We'd ply him with tequila shots (don't tell UPS!) as we became a fraternity of ambition and insanity. We had our sights set on grand success as we shipped off our babies to forward-thinking customers. We were going to change the world, or at least the speaker world.

We quickly outgrew my garage, and I had to rent a small industrial space. But we kept expanding, forcing me to negotiate with Charlie, our landlord, to let us take sledgehammers to the wall, breaking through to the next unit. Then months later, it happened again, then again, until there just weren't any more units. We had to move to a much bigger space, and then we repeated the break-through-walls routine until we took over the entire building. By that point, we were fifty people building hundreds of speakers every week. I had gone from start-up idea guy to CEO of a legitimate company with people, payroll, HR, shareholders, taxes, insurance, a hundred vendors, shippers, assembly lines, test labs, and thankfully, hundreds of dealers and customers around the world. But all this meant there was very little time for me to be the visionary, creative idea guy. Actually, what happened is I had to shift my creativity to marketing, sales, management, and operations. Designing new products had to happen at night. There's a lesson in here somewhere.

Maybe it's that success doesn't happen overnight, and it's always harder than you expect.

In the early days of any business, initial sales are always critical—and exciting. In the case of commercial speakers for large open ceilings, those first sales also required hair-raising installations. Extension ladders and entrepreneurial exuberance—it's not that different from drunk driving. Dangerous, outrageous, no control, and guess what: I got to be the guy on the ladder. No one else in our early crew wanted to go up, drill holes in I-beams, or wire and hang heavy and awkward speakers. Scary stuff, but we needed every install we could get for credibility, photos, and marketing promotions, not to mention dollars.

Another requirement of most product companies is the trade show, a chance to expose your new, and hopefully novel, product to professional buyers in a specific industry. The first SoundTube trade show we scheduled was in Chicago, and we didn't even have finished products. So we did what any self-respecting, young, and eager company would do: we worked around the clock for days, hooked my Suburban to a jam-packed U-Haul, and hit the road. After a twenty-four-hour drive, four of us arrived at a winter-cold convention center. (Conference halls don't waste heat while exhibitors are busy doing setup). For us, this first setup was fraught with stress, particularly the moment when we extended all the newly assembled SoundTubes. As the flexible tubes got stretched out to their desired length, we heard a sickening sound: the snap of the wires being pulled off their terminals inside the tubes. It turned out our audio engineering expert on the team hadn't wanted to waste wire, so he cut the lengths to what he thought would be "just right," common sense be damned. Unfortunately, he didn't consider that flexible tubes are just that, *flexible*. After too many hours of work, driving, and more work, we were faced with disassembling all the SoundTubes. I think we finally left the convention center around 3:00 a.m., exhausted and off to a great start.

As time went on, the product evolved, as did our manufacturing methods. We went from enclosures made of flexible rubber hose to rotational-molded plastic to compression-molded composite to injection-molded composite. It was exciting stuff, redesigning the product and developing increasingly advanced components. About every two years, we launched a whole new product line, and this evolution showed the industry and its top customers that we were serious. We were focused on constant innovation to improve sonic performance, sound coverage, installation ease and style. It worked. We won business with national and international chains over Bose, JBL, and other major brands. Along the way, I developed a tic, an unconscious habit, of looking skyward anytime I walked into a store, restaurant, or airport to see whose speakers were installed. I was fully committed to my mission to convert the world.

Part of our unique approach to exposing our novel products was to find ways to make a splash without spending money we didn't have. One such marketing moment was when I talked auto-racing friend Gerry Jackson into letting me cover his race car with SoundTube graphics. He was racing a Ferrari in the IMSA GT Series and already had his costs covered. I designed a cool livery for him and we made the most of the resulting photos. Our dealers ate it up. Our small company suddenly appeared to be big time. (We never mentioned it only cost us the decals.) Of course, it wasn't suddenly all easy sailing. In fact, there wasn't any easy sailing.

People make the company, and yet like many start-ups, we didn't have the budget for normal salaries. We had to hire the lowest-cost people we could find and then turn them into something. Along the way, I had to deal with drunk or hungover salespeople at tradeshows, crooks, and jailbirds. Sadly, this wasn't limited to our staff. We also had suspect dealers, reps, and distributors, along with vendors and others on the take.

Oh, and then there was the time when we had finally started selling real volume and our director of sales decided it would make sense to pretend he was CEO and offer crazy pricing and insider info to entice a major dealer. That led to his firing and my having to do serious damage control to save the account after I learned they'd black-balled our company based on his slimy practices. And once again, I had to use creative genius to plot revenge on this guy.

The stories go on and on, but the key takeaway is that personnel management is the most critical element of any business. Payroll is your biggest expense, and no business can afford to make too many mistakes. Track your team's work and behavior, and don't ever be afraid to fire. It's incredibly hard the first time—especially for key people—but trust your gut and get rid of the bad actors. You will actually feel really good once it's done.

Thankfully, most of our personnel were good people who shared some great moments. We celebrated many of them with little things like parking lot street hockey games in the middle of the workday, BBQ lunches at the office, and trophies for every million dollars a salesperson sold. There was also the ringing of a ship's bell for every large order, Indian food fests, martini-fueled office parties, Olympic bobsled rides, and other treats. All of this fun stuff fell under "team building," though it just came to us naturally. It wasn't calculated, and it came long before the internet and Silicon Valley's bean-bag-chair, free-dry-cleaning, and unlimited-mocha-latte explosion.

Here's another highlight: Ferrari called. I got pulled out of a critical engineering meeting with a university acoustics lab. There was a call, and I was told I needed to take it. I was fearing the worst, but then I heard who was on the line. "Ferrari is calling? Really?" Amazing!

They wanted to talk to me about creating a custom speaker for their international auto show display, starting with the North American International Show in New York City. To add even more excitement to this dream job, they also wanted me to create a second series of custom speakers for their gala party event planned for the first evening of the New York show. This was big!

You can probably imagine how I reacted to this request. Can you say, "One-track mind"? I dug in and spent time planning, designing, and ultimately leaving the office regularly to work in my new private workshop in the studio I'd built next to my house. I felt a connection to Ferrari again. I was proud. I was over the moon. I had to make the most of this.

In the end, the speakers were beautiful, and all of Ferrari's displays looked great. I flew into Manhattan to supervise the installation and, more importantly, to shoot about eight hundred rolls of film. Little did I know that a couple of years later, I'd go all in with Ferrari on a far more involved audio program.

As our business and products evolved, I kept pushing for better performance and more meaningful features—the things that listeners, audiovisual personnel, and customers would appreciate: higher sound quality, ease of installation, affordability, and availability. We had been selling lots of speakers, all built in our facility in Park City, but to truly advance the quality and performance of our products, we needed the talent and vertical manufacturing capabilities available only in Asia. I say this having tried and tried and tried to find a domestic supplier who could make what I was dreaming up. It was time to commit and go for a turnkey solution—a fully built, tested, packaged, and shipped product that we would not touch except for visual reviews and spot testing.

We had a few contacts at factories in China, so I scheduled a trip for three of us to see, meet, audit, and hopefully commit to one factory. I was doing all this with plans in my head of a brand-new line of speakers that would provide the best sound of any commercial speaker on the market, make installation much faster and more secure, and raise aesthetics, fit, and finish to a new level.

I guess now is a good time for my diatribe on China and "Made in the USA." We often hear Americans pooh-poohing Asian products and production. They claim everything should be made in the US, they'll only buy American, and American businesses can make perfectly good products at home and never miss a beat. They are *wrong*. These "experts" make a lot of noise, but they have little real experience. Except for some specific industries, it's just wrong. For electronics, it's pretty much impossible.

It's not that I am anti-American. I'm pro-American. I just know enough about manufacturing to know that it's generally impossible to efficiently mass-produce complex audio and electronic products in America. And it's because we don't have factories with vertical capabilities.

Factories in the United States typically do one thing. They have one process and one specialty. It might be injection molding, machining, plating, painting, sewing, circuit board stuffing, assembly, printing, or packaging, but in Asia, lots of factories can do all these things—right under one roof. For manufacturers like SoundTube and so many others, who can't possibly afford to set up their own factories, production moves to Asia because they simply can't produce their products in the United States. Relying on US production would make the products so expensive no one would buy them. It would also mean organizing and coordinating dozens, if not hundreds, of suppliers, and then waiting as each performed their portion of the process at great operational and transport expense.

Time and efficiency aren't the only reasons it's next to impossible to make many complex mass-produced products in the United States. Quality—yes, *quality*—is another major aspect of this misunderstood manufacturing myth. When I created our most advanced line of SoundTube speakers, there wasn't a US company that could achieve the quality we required. Sure, US suppliers might be able to make some of the parts, but the quality, consistency, and cost would be all over the place. Our decision to make turnkey speakers in China allowed me to design the best, highest quality products possible with the features, fit, and finish that would impress and satisfy our customers. Try to imagine this: our Chinese factory was making custom woofers and tweeters to our specifications, custom circuit boards, injection molded enclosures, die-cast metal parts to our drawings, specially formed metal grilles, custom molded rubber parts, special wire harnesses, transformers, switches and knobs with our logos and markings, and dozens of other specialized parts for each of our multiple products, along with custom formed and beautifully printed boxes along with custom molded liners so that each SoundTube would be perfectly cradled as it travelled to its ultimate destination around the globe, but not before it was assembled, inspected and tested. Put a different way, we were able to offer a far better product at the same price as our prior US-made products, giving our customers a significantly better offering and experience.

My last word on the Asia issue is this: What's more important, having a US company making its products domestically and losing market share or going out of business because its products can't compete, or have a US company succeeding by selling products it has made in Asia? Think of the jobs lost versus the long term hiring. Think of the taxes paid by these two companies. Which makes more sense?

For the record, one of our ventures in the cyber-encryption space, 7Tunnels, required us to make our products, including software, circuit boards, and so on, in the United States. Why? Because this is a high-security product. It has to be manufactured in the US to ensure that no unusual software bugs or circuits are snuck into the goods. On an even scarier note, the quantum-resistant data encryption technology we created and patented is considered a weapon by the Department of Defense. It can't be shared or sold internationally without significant—*significant*—regulation and approval. The fact that our tech can protect data from decryption by even quantum computers makes it one of the more powerful weapons on the planet, if used improperly. So you see, I'm equal opportunity.

Back to our story. The trip to China to review factories resulted in a clear choice that could help SoundTube make better products and continue to grow. I would need to get board approval for this kind of move, so I scheduled a board meeting, knowing I'd need to do a lot of educating. I spent a week preparing my information, data, projections, and other presentation materials.

The three board members flew in. I was prepared. We had amazing new product designs, a complete cost analysis, performance comparisons, and more. I had my stuff, our CFO's presentation, and Peter Metcalf, founder and CEO of Black Diamond mountaineering equipment, who would provide a third-party testimonial on the merits of Asian production.

Two of the three board members understood and believed in what we were saying, but they deferred to their leader, who had his own beliefs about Asia, most of them based on political or sensationalized stories and media. He ended with, "I'll think about it, but I don't like it. For now, it's a no." What I haven't mentioned is the fact that I'd been driving this effort for months. I knew the numbers and the timelines to get product in-house. I knew that every week we delayed pushing the Go button would have a major impact on our revenue and bottom line. We'd weathered a "you need to close the doors" event a year earlier, and I wasn't going to let that happen again. We had survived that dreadful moment, and like a phoenix, we rose out of the mess and kept rising with new products, better performance, new customers, and a never-say-die attitude. It was amazing. I was confident the board meeting would be a formality. I was wrong—but there would be no turning back for me. Our China commitment would turn SoundTube into the company and brand we all wanted it to be.

Now might be a good time to give you a sense of just how important all of this really was to me and how much I had been through to get to this point, before I tell you the rest of the SoundTube story.

As a serial entrepreneur, working in many industries and in many roles, I've encountered not only all kinds of people and projects but also all kinds of highs and lows. In order to truly paint the entire picture of what life as an entrepreneur, businessperson, and creative guy is like, it's incumbent upon me to make sure you get the unvarnished truth—warts and all, as people like to say. It's impossible to paint this picture without also being willing to sprinkle in some very personal details and some tidbits about my family life. As much as I try to keep my family out of my business and shield them from the most difficult aspects of life as a risk-taker, I have to remind myself that there's a constant physical and emotional dynamic that impacts my work, and vice versa.

Nothing that follows is written to elicit sympathy or concern or dramatize my life. This is simply the recounting of some of the realities and experiences that I have waded through on my long, strange trip—a trip that is far from over. In fact, even though I have survived these moments and have put them to paper, I still ride the emotional roller coaster daily as I create new products and new ventures. It doesn't end just because a book gets written.

What I hope to achieve here is to help others make good and smart decisions as they travel on their own entrepreneurial journey—or in the case of parents, friends, children, and advisors of a budding risk-taker, to help them recognize the signs and find ways to encourage, support, help, and in some cases stop, the child or person in question.

It can be the worst stress you will ever know. For me, in my entrepreneurial adventure, driving off a cliff wasn't a euphemism. It was real. There were so many moments when the stress and struggle seemed insurmountable. Money flowing out faster than in. People to take care of at work and at home. Banks and investors to satisfy. It was beyond overwhelming.

Ninety-eight percent of all humans are never going to take the full entrepreneurial challenge, and they are never going to lay it all on the line for their work. For this reason, they will never understand the risk, fear, and hopeful rewards. This also means they are never going to be able to help you. Advisors, supporters, and therapists will never be 100 percent effective. They might try, but they can't really offer solid help if they've never undertaken similar activities. I couldn't get it from my wife or family. I couldn't get it from most of my friends. I couldn't get it from my crew at work—after all, I had to be a leader. Tough. Resilient. Impervious to problems. *Bulletproof.* The fact is, most of the time, I felt alone. I had to bury the fear, hide the stress, never show weakness. My SoundTube Thanksgiving breakdown was a moment when I exposed my real self. Then, after committing to going along with the family trip plans, it was all but forgotten by Kate and the kids. They moved quickly past it while I suffered inside. I had to be the leader of my family. No room for wobbly knees.

The problem with carrying the load of entrepreneurial, business, and financial stress all by yourself is that it gnaws at you. You go to bed an invisible wreck, hoping to wake up and fix it all. It's a roller coaster of extremes, but in between, during middle-of-the-night waking moments, when no one is asking you for help, answers, money, time, or whatever else, you sink into the black hole of suicidal resolution. At least I did. Often.

When I got on that plane to Connecticut, I had more than a passing thought about how lovely it would be if the plane went down and I could put it all behind me.

This may not be your idea of nice, but this is the true stuff. Pressure and time are what create geological events. In the case of the human psyche, pressure and time can cause a mental version of liquid hot magma that flows through your brain and body. It causes headaches, backaches, and much worse. The real issue is how you manage these volcanic moments. Maybe harder than being an entrepreneur is being the bodyguard for your own entrepreneurship. Learning to focus on the next exciting moment and striving to achieve that next goal became my recipe for bulletproofing myself against my own negative ideas. Thankfully, my passion won out.

Back to our story.

The China presentation concluded and the SoundTube board of directors left, flying home on their private jet. I stayed at work, licking my wounds and strategizing. After rehashing all the day's events with Peter and my CFO, Clarke, I made a critical move. I knew what was right. What was best for everyone involved. I called Hendrik, our Chinese factory point person in California, and told him to get on a plane that night. If we were going to hit our targets, we needed him in China the next day, delivering the design files and the go-ahead to start tooling up. This was no minor decision. I was pushing my agenda and knew the board would freak out. But I couldn't wait for them to "decide." I told Hendrik the whole story, then I told him I'd cover all the expenses incurred if the board shut me down at a later date. This was going to be the most impressive launch in the history of the company.

I blatantly disregarded the board, and as it turned out, we created impressive new products. Our reps and dealers loved them, our launch was amazing, and the customers were thrilled. In the end, the board was also thrilled, with claims of "Gee, it sure is good we decided to go to China" and other bizarre comments. My favorite: "The next time you travel to China, let us know so we can join you, and maybe we can bring our kids." Bring our kids? This was business, not a field trip! And by the way, they never said yes.

I need to make it clear that I do not suggest you disregard your board or make decisions on your own when you are bound to a company charter. Working with your board, and others generally, is critical in business. It's also a skill—it doesn't just happen. Of course, it's not easy to take the high road when others think it's time for the off-ramp. I chose to take a risk by moving our production to China—a calculated risk—and it paid off. I got lucky.

The growth of SoundTube was painfully slow in the early days, but then it was meteoric—at least for an audio company—as we doubled sales our second year, then tripled, then doubled sales again, matching my original business plan exactly. This is unusual, as projections are rarely accurate, but I forced our team to live by, and hit, our numbers. We used a daily sales report to track every person's activity and overall sales to ensure the team knew exactly where we stood. That sheet was a torturous taskmaster, but it worked. Our problem was rapid growth—often the undoing of a growing business—and we almost went under due to impossible cash-flow issues. But we survived and then launched the turnkey speaker products made in the Chinese factory, which were a big hit. But it wasn't all good news.

Sometimes honesty, directness, experience, and vision just aren't enough to keep business relationships alive. I'd been managing the new version of SoundTube—which included a new investor, new board, new Florida warehouse facility, new product line, and new Chinese production—for about a year and a half, when it became obvious that our new investor wanted to throw his weight around. I had been doing a good job of running the company I founded, creating new designs, building up our dealer base, increasing our marketing efforts and media exposure, growing sales and international business, and all the other things that a rapidly growing company wants and needs. We were on a great track, and our resellers and international distributors loved what was happening. The only person who wasn't in love was our new investor. He'd come in with a huge amount of funding and now held fifty-one percent—the magic number. He'd loved everything about SoundTube when he came on, and things had only gotten better, including that big move to Chinese production. Then, suddenly, he started flexing his fifty-one percent muscles and demanded inefficient operational changes.

It wasn't long before my frustration with his new attitude got jacked up a notch. Now he wanted to be CEO. What? We'd agreed I'd remain CEO when he'd invested his money. I was the founder and had been CEO from day one. I'd managed the company through all kinds of ups and downs, and now we were poised for greatness. That didn't seem to matter. It also didn't seem to matter that our company was in Park City and he was based in the mid-west.

That's what happens. People let their personal interests, egos, and unrelated business ideas of how the world should work cloud their thinking. That doesn't mean their ideas are automatically wrong. What it means is that, once again, they should be open and honest about the realities of their talents, knowledge, and experience. And so should I.

Things started to become clear to me. We had a problem. I had a problem. Then it got worse. I was told by Mr. Fifty-One Percent that I'd have one of "his people" shadowing me and monitoring our progress. The over-the-hill "expert" he saddled me with exhibited classic old-guy behaviors that were so painfully obvious it was laughable. He wanted to show me the power of his new position from the very start, hitting me with the classics: "Do you know who I am?" and "Do you know how much I just spent on my house?" It was basically, do you know how important I think I am? I was embarrassed for him. He had no experience with our industry. He had no hands-on knowledge. He was just a self-important old man trying to exhibit relevance. *Relevance.* It's what self-proclaimed experts past their prime are searching for. Whether they were ever experts or not, they all too often get older, do a bit less, then less and less, and then they're mostly about convincing new encounters that they *are* someone rather than *being* someone.

This guy was there to make changes, not to improve things but to show his power. There was no way I was going to tolerate him. He was a micromanager and a Monday-morning quarterback, and he was messing with my people. That was the final straw.

No, this was the final straw: I was informed Mr. Fifty-One Percent would now have to approve *all* expenses. And this wasn't a simple approval request; he required a seven-item checklist of details for each expenditure. This was management insanity. The only bright spot: the very first purchase we *desired* after this new mandate was for toilet seat protective paper covers. You know, those tissue paper horseshoes you place on the toilet seat to protect your butt. Our purchase order totaled about six dollars. Imagine having your purchasing department write a seven-point request for toilet seat tissues. I was done!

I laid it out for Mr. Fifty-One Percent: "Either I buy you out or you buy me out." It didn't take long. He agreed to pay me, and I agreed that it was best for both parties. There was no way we'd ever work well together given the "management" methods he wanted to employ. My only real concern at that point was my other shareholders. All I could do was appeal to Mr. Fifty-One Percent to treat the original investors fairly and respect the fact that they'd played a key role in making SoundTube a reality.

We figured out the paperwork and payment, and that was that. A few weeks later, I was walking out of SoundTube, a company, brand, and product line I'd created from nothing. They tied me to a two-year consulting agreement, but that was just window dressing to keep the industry and our dealers calm. I was mentally out.

SoundTube continues to make its products in Asia these twenty years later, and quite successfully. My work with SoundTube and the things I created there have made a global (no kidding) impact on the design and quality of sound in the commercial audio world. In fact, the impact has been so great that major brands, including JBL, Bose, Crestron, and others have copied my designs so carefully that I often think I'm seeing SoundTubes when they are actually copycat products. Damn tic . . .

On the day I walked out of SoundTube for the last time, I already had ideas about my next move. I had been dreaming about creating a statement audio product. Something that would dazzle eyes and ears. Time to contact Ferrari.

CHAPTER 9
NOW WHAT?

I HADN'T FULLY SATISFIED MY DRIVE to push the limits in audio. SoundTube speakers were innovative and impressive in their design, performance, ease of installation, and customer impact, but they were speakers for retail stores, restaurants, and public spaces, not the types of settings where one expects to unleash "the ultimate" in performance and style. But if the audio industry had so many landmines and sketchy folks, why in hell would I jump right back in? Ferrari, that's why!

During my last couple of years at SoundTube, I had thought about a killer speaker product I codenamed Secret Weapon. It was time to show off. Not in the typical show-off sense of the word but as in "Let's show off all we've learned and create the ultimate speaker product." I'd been marinating in Ferrari since I was five, and I'd already created unique SoundTube speakers for Ferrari's commercial events. Now it was time to go Formula One on the speaker world, and Ferrari was the perfect partner for such an assault on the *consumer* audio industry.

I set my wheels in motion and started sketching out something that addressed both the key elements of great sound and the details that would appeal to lovers of luxury, quality, and performance—that is, Ferrari types! My years of passion and involvement with Ferrari gave me direct insight into the mindset and culture of Ferrari's fans, customers, and corporate sensibilities. I wanted this new product to scream "wow" and cement in the minds of audio and Ferrari fanatics that David Wiener Ventures creates the ultimate products for people who love design and high performance. Now all I had to do was pitch—and convince—Ferrari. That's all …

It's not like you just call up Ferrari and say, "Hi, guys, I've got a great idea." They can work with anyone they want, and they don't talk to anyone unless they truly want to. I went through my contacts from the Ferrari, Formula One, and motorsports worlds trying to figure out a way in. I ended up calling a guy I'd bought a Ferrari F1 car body from. Andrew knew some people at Ferrari, and when I explained my plan, he said he'd make a call and suggested I fly to Maranello, where someone would meet with me. He sounded only mildly convincing. I worried and sweated as I made my flight and hotel plans. It felt like Vegas odds: travel to Italy for a week without any idea if and when I'd get an audience with someone of consequence.

After a lot of designing, prototyping, and drafting marketing and sales plans, I still didn't have an answer to my question: Would I get my meeting to show the fancy presentation I'd created? But there I was in Maranello, the sacred land of Ferrari. I had no schedule, no plans, nothing, wondering when and how I'd find out if I'd get a meeting. I just had to hope and wait, wait and hope. Franco, the manager of Hotel Planet, was used to hosting Ferraristas who'd come to pay homage to one of the true Italian religions, but he took a special liking to me, appreciating that I was there on real business, not tourist stuff. He fed me espressos followed by cappuccinos—clearly the worst diet for someone sitting around nervously waiting, and waiting some more. I had to do something else. I was wired.

I decided to wander about town, trying to preoccupy myself and take my mind off the burning question: Would there be a message light on when I got back to my room? After three days, I was beginning to think I should reschedule my flight home and save some money. Then, the next day, I got a call. *The* call. My hotel phone rang. They said yes—I had a meeting. Could I be there at 10:00 a.m. tomorrow? With stress levels at the redline, the idea of finally getting to meet was almost scary. Would I be wound so tight I'd blurt out something stupid or not present all the information I'd prepared? Could I be there? Hell yes!

My presentation struck a chord with the higher-ups at Ferrari. They realized I had distilled a forty-year love affair with Ferrari and all that I'd learned about Ferrari's cars, products, people, image, and branding not to mention, Ferrari culture, into a carefully crafted statement on design, performance, and luxury. I had captured the essence of Ferrari life, Ferrari thinking, Ferrari culture, and the Ferrari market. I'd probably put more thought into *Ferrari* than most of them—really—and suddenly, my education was shining through. They were impressed. My proposal worked, and I was invited back for a second meeting a few months later to present a prototype of my Ferrari Art.Engine.

On my next trip, I brought one of my audio engineers with me. Flight regulations required that any piece of luggage had to be one hundred pounds or less. Given that the prototype was finished in the wee hours before our flight and weighed in at about 110 pounds, we had to strip out all the electronics in order to make weight. This also required that I spend 1:00 a.m. to 3:00 a.m. sewing an ultralightweight protective travel case—normal packaging would be far too heavy. The prototype was four feet of beautifully machined aluminum, and it could not get hurt!

At the airport later that morning, I'd made weight—almost. The ticket lady indicated that the whole thing weighed 101 pounds. I assured her it did not and that their scale was off. She assured me my machine was not going to Italy. I asked for her supervisor and suffered all her facial gyrations until she finally acquiesced. I pleaded my case, doing my best Perry Mason, and was able to convince her that the atomic scales we used at our Ferrari fabrication facility were government certified and that the Delta scale was clearly off and needed to be recalibrated. Thankfully she bought my BS, and we made it to Maranello.

Hours later, I was back in Italy, with my room at Hotel Planet quickly turned into an assembly facility. We'd put the final screws back into the reassembled Art.Engine, and with a gratifying click, my audio engineer pushed the Engine Start button on the gleaming aluminum tower. BOOM—the room went dark. No power. Damn.

As it turned out, my engineer had messed up the internal power connection, causing a massive short, thankfully to the hotel (am I seriously saying this?) and not to the Art.Engine. The entire Hotel Planet was in the dark, no power anywhere. Lucky for me, my friendship with the manager, Franco, had been built on his respect for all things Ferrari. He was very forgiving and went out to the street to find the power main while I, with only minutes before the local stores in this tiny town were going to close, had to jump in my car and hunt down miscellaneous electrical bits. You can't imagine how hard it was to talk shopkeepers into opening their locked doors as I tried to talk—and draw—my way to them understanding what I needed. It took three stores before I got the necessary electrical connectors and other odd items. I returned to my room triumphant, hoping we would confirm that the Art.Engine was not damaged by the power surge. I crossed my fingers as the sweating engineer fiddled and finalized the connections. Click. BOOM. Blackness, again.

I had to go back downstairs, tail between my legs, and convince Franco that we were not trying to sabotage his hotel. Thankfully, his good nature and support of my work outweighed his concern for all the other guests, and he once again headed outside to throw the main.

Upon returning to my room, Mr. Twice Failed delighted in telling me that he had forgotten to reverse the flux capacitor or some other techno gibberish. With me holding my breath, and him knowing his life was at stake, he hit the button. The Art.Engine lit up and worked perfectly, all 110 pounds of it.

The next day I was to present the Art.Engine in all its glory to the decision-makers at Ferrari. This was a huge meeting for me, the culmination of everything I'd worked for, everything I'd stressed over. We made it safely to Director Zambeletti's office and placed the Art.Engine prototype near one wall. There were several Ferrari people in the room, all dressed like pages out of an Italian fashion magazine. A bit daunting. Actually, all of it was daunting. A new (and unproven) product concept, a new potential partnership, new people to deal with, international business, laws, finance, and taxes to figure out, and a major manufacturing commitment on my part if Ferrari said yes. All the while, I couldn't help wondering whether the Art.Engine was actually wired properly. Would we black out all of Ferrari? That would be popular . . .

Then I was informed that Jean Todt himself, the new CEO of Ferrari and the celebrated director of Ferrari's Formula One team, with a string of consecutive F1 World Championship titles to his name, would be stopping by to give his blessing (or not) to this proposed partnership. I was told that he was a very busy man and that I'd only get two minutes. TWO MINUTES?! I was told to not ask questions and keep my answers short. Daunting doesn't begin to describe it . . .

Jean Todt was ushered into the office by one of his assistants. Quick introductions all around. *Remember, keep it brief.* Jean Todt turned out to be a music lover and asked a lot of questions about the Art.Engine, about me, and the proposed partnership. Then he asked to light up the Art.Engine so he could hear it rock. I was doing my best to keep my responses brief, and I could see the evil eyeballs I was getting from across the room. My handlers were probably thinking their careers were on the line if Mr. Todt was late for his next meeting.

Mr. Todt ended up talking with me for at least twenty minutes. Everyone was nervous and worried—everyone but Jean Todt and me. I was loving this. Time with one of the most accomplished motorsports and automotive leaders in the world, and he was talking to me! He loved it. The Art.Engine. The sound. The design. The art of it all.

He eventually left, and I could feel the tension in the room as the Ferrari people looked at each other, then at me, as if I'd made him stay. The meeting had been a great success. Now on to the contract phase!

Back home, I started hunting for a suitable commercial space to manufacture these audio monsters. As I say about all products, they don't just happen. It takes a lot of work to create and make a product. In this case, we were doing product development, designing and producing every aspect of the Art.Engine, from the machined billet aluminum enclosure to the electronics, amps, circuitry, wireless music delivery system, and speaker driver details, down to the decals on the back of each three-inch woofer proclaiming the DWV and Ferrari partnership. Then there was the Ferrari paint process, the hundreds of tiny bits, odds and ends, and all the plating, anodizing, polishing, and other insanely detailed items required to produce *just one* Art.Engine. That wasn't all. We also needed to design, source, and order custom-made wood crates to ship the solid aluminum audio systems in a way that would ensure not even a tiny scratch or ding. In case you think that's simple, there are even regulations about the type of wood you have to use, among other things, to prevent insects from hitching a ride from one country to another!

All this stuff was happening while I hunted for shop space. When I finally found the right place, there was yet another contract and the inevitable personal guarantee. This is the way banks, landlords, and suppliers lock you in so regardless of what happens to your budding business, they ensure their payment while simultaneously ensuring you sleepless nights. I signed. Here we go again . . .

I'd made a lot of commitments along the way to see this project through, but the biggest—at least I thought so at the time—was purchasing two very large HAAS CNC milling machines to turn huge blocks of raw aluminum into elegant, sculpted shapes, complete with precise pockets, slots, threaded holes, reinforcing channels, and sound wave barriers. This was truly Formula One. Machines used to make F1 components, rocket parts, and other precision products were going to make DWV Ferrari Art.Engines. In-house! The bar was being raised daily.

Part of the process involved cementing our business association with Ferrari. Perhaps I was guilty of putting the cart before the horse, but I was confident we'd have a solid agreement based on Jean Todt's enthusiasm for the Art.Engine. After going a few rounds with Ferrari's lawyers, we finally had a contract and simultaneously began full production.

As Ferrari Art.Engines started shipping around the world, along with glowing magazine reviews, Ferrari got more excited and more involved. I decided Jean Todt deserved a real thank-you, so I shipped him a black Art.Engine. *Nero*, as Ferrari black is known, turned out to be the right choice, as every Ferrari he owned was black. It was the right thing to do—a free $20,000 gift. Jean invited me to his home outside Paris to unveil it. He had me picked up at Charles de Gaulle airport by a Ferrari driver, then gave me a day of fine food and wine. Eating outside, surrounded by modern sculptures, motorsports memorabilia, and a group of his close friends, it was a magical setting.

This was an opportunity for me to get to know Jean Todt a bit, learn about his life outside of motorsports, learn what made him tick, and understand more about why a powerhouse like Ferrari would put a Frenchman in charge of its most prized possession. As director of their Formula One team and CEO of the entire company, Jean Todt was already a legend. Through uncanny team development and performance, he'd elevated F1 star Michael Schumacher to superstar status, helping him win five consecutive World Championships, starting in 2000—unheard of and particularly amazing given the fact that, before Jean Todt, Ferrari's last Formula One World Championship winner was Jody Scheckter in 1979.

After lunch, dessert, photos, and many shared stories, it was time to leave. Jean Todt was a gracious host and continued his generosity with an invitation to ride back to Paris with him. As we traveled, he asked me about the treatment I was receiving from Ferrari's international distributors. He specifically asked what kind of support I was receiving from Ferrari North America. I mentioned that they hadn't really done anything to date. And that was all it took. He got out his mobile phone and dialed the CEO of Ferrari North America (FNA), Maurizio Parlato, even though it was Sunday. He knew Maurizio was going to pick up the phone instantly, regardless of the day or time. Jean gave Maurizio an earful and demanded that FNA make some major action happen for me and the Art.Engine. By the time he was finished, Jean told me FNA was going to arrange a premiere event at its Park Avenue showroom in New York City, invite me to present the Art.Engine at the LA Auto Show, and champion other helpful efforts. It was one of those wow moments when you think you are dreaming but it's real. Then it got better.

I was scheduled to fly to Maranello the following day for meetings at Ferrari. I had my ticket on Alitalia, and I had a plan to get out of Paris on a schedule that would ensure I didn't risk missing my flight. Jean asked me about my work schedule, and when he heard I was headed to Ferrari, he immediately asked me to fly with him on the Ferrari corporate jet rather than go commercial. For him, it wasn't about the luxury. He was a performance guy, and he knew I'd be more productive and enjoy the rare opportunity of flying with him. This was a Ferrari lover's dream come true: to travel on the Ferrari jet with the company's CEO and director of the F1 team. Dream on!

Landing at Bologna airport, we were ushered from our private spot on the tarmac into the terminal. Walking along, I experienced the respect and awe that the Italians had for this giant of motorsports. The double-takes were endless, and the staring was laser-like. For my part, I got to enjoy the thrill of being Jean's sole travel companion (ignoring his security personnel). This surreal Ferrari adventure ended with Jean having his driver take me to my hotel—again, Hotel Planet across from the factory—after a quick stop at Jean's home on the outskirts of Maranello. The next day would be more exciting business at Ferrari. I was truly living my dream.

I was consumed in the following months with how to manufacture a limited edition, one-thousand-piece run of our high-precision and painstakingly painted and assembled DWV Ferrari Art.Engines in a rainbow of Ferrari colors. We shipped Art Engines to moguls and movie stars, F1 pilots, and Ferrari fanatics, luxury hotels and resorts. In the end, Ferrari wrote to me that the Art.Engine was the first true piece of art Ferrari had ever offered. You can imagine how that made me feel. Their director of brand development at the time, Giulio Zambeletti, stated, "Any high-end product licensed by Ferrari must have an uncompromising approach to quality, breakthrough technology, and ultimate performance. The Art. Engine encompasses them all."

The press was equally enthusiastic in articles written all over the world. At the time, Brent Butterworth, editor-in-chief for *Home Entertainment* magazine and the industry guru of audio quality, wrote, "One look and you know you're confronting a music system like no other ever created. [DWV] have succeeded far beyond what I believed possible from such an unconventional design. I cannot think of a more realistic-sounding speaker than this one, save perhaps a few extremely high-end speakers from Goldmund and a few others. The Art.Engine embodies what every high-end product should: dazzling looks, dependable performance, and simplicity of design and operation. They got this one right—it deserves to wear the Ferrari logo."

With great press, happy Ferrari executives in Italy and around the globe, and a beautiful product to look at daily, there were many more good moments than bad. Overall, the Ferrari partnership, Ferrari Art. Engine product, and the excitement it generated made this a fantastically satisfying project. The housing crisis and subsequent economic downturn did impact us along the way, but all the speed bumps were worth it in the end. Working with a brand you dreamed about as a kid and still hold in high regard as an adult is singularly amazing. Rare at best and almost impossible to repeat, our business and design association with Ferrari was a dream career moment. Then I went over the edge.

I never should have done it. I wish I hadn't. Excitement and a bit of ego got the better of me. This move would take a toll on me. On my business. On the music-loving world.

I was deep into the Ferrari Art.Engine project when a business associate planted a seed. There was a company called Aphex, in the pro audio market, making gear for recording studios and concert venues, and they were famous for audio processing technology. The idea was that perhaps we could get Aphex processing into the Ferrari Art.Engine to make it sound even better. We shipped an Art.Engine to California so the Aphex engineers could mock up a circuit for us to test. The improvement in sound was significant. The price would turn out to be another story.

As I got used to the new and improved sound of the Art.Engine, my gears started to spin. Why not apply this tech to all kinds of products? I signed what seemed like a crazy licensing deal: $10,000 a month for exclusive rights to use Aphex tech in any and all consumer products. It was a huge number. If only I'd stopped there.

As time rolled on and we developed our relationship with Aphex, it became obvious that they wanted to sell the business. Their tech was a staple used on almost every great record album or at every major music event produced over the previous twenty years. It wasn't long before we were scheming ways to buy the whole business and take Aphex into the consumer market. I believed in this so much that, while I worked to raise investment funds, I mortgaged our home so I could meet the purchase deadline. Not great for a marriage!

My goal for Aphex was to get its powerhouse technology into all kinds of audio devices, including through licensing for consumer products. It was so obvious: an easy-to-integrate, low-cost way to have a huge impact on sonic performance. How could this not be a slam dunk? Let me tell you.

There was another thing I had to learn the hard (and expensive) way as I plotted the global improvement of the music world. Most manufacturers don't license other people's technology for one reason: ego. They don't want to use things that aren't created in-house. They suffer from NIH (not invented here) syndrome. They're afraid of ever admitting that someone else—someone outside their hallowed offices—may have created something great or, at the very least, something useful.

As we worked at licensing our Aphex technology to help audio manufacturers make their products sound better, I was repeatedly shocked and let down at how chicken so many respectable companies were: Monster, Klipsch, Apple, Skullcandy, Bose, and more. We demonstrated our tech to all of these companies. They all agreed the performance benefit was dramatic. They all agreed the cost was reasonable. They all agreed that the marketing opportunity was powerful. But they all chickened out under a cloud of NIH.

I remember my last licensing sales call. I traveled to Framingham, Massachusetts, to present our tech to the lead engineer on Bose's then-latest-and-greatest portable speaker. I stopped at BestBuy the day before and purchased their new, bestselling product. I drove to the meeting. I sat down with this engineer and played their device with a piece of music chosen by him. His product sounded fine (*fine* is not a compliment). I then played the same piece and applied the Aphex sonic processing, pressing an On/Off button so he could instantly compare the impact of our technology on his own. He was clearly moved by the dramatic improvement to his product. He looked me in the eyes and said it was amazing, and the cost was a nonissue. Then he said Bose had no need for it. He shook my hand, led me out, and that was the end of it. But that was not the end of it for me.

Around 2012, I had become zealous about the idea of bringing higher quality listening experiences to the world of consumer audio and anyone who loved music—like, only a zillion people. I was not into audiophile insanity, but rather real-world, good sound based on the original work artists had created in the studio. It continued to baffle me that musicians spent countless hours, days, weeks—even months—tweaking the sound of their recordings, only to have half the detail lost in the downgraded digital music files iTunes, Pandora, Spotify, and others were making the standard of the day.

As the impact of the iPod, iPhone, and apps became ubiquitous, I figured maybe the best way to get our technology, and the benefits it could offer, to the masses was by creating our own app. All we had to do was figure out how to turn our extraordinary piece of professional recording gear into a digital app. How hard could it be? If I could just make this app a reality, I could change the world of music.

As we were working on the new app, music legend and audio quality curmudgeon Neil Young was making a big play by launching his new digital audio system, Pono, for the consumer music world. He had spent years railing against the quality of CDs and digital music, making all kinds of assertions and claims. His reputation as sonic-quality protector of the universe preceded him. His team created a Toblerone-like hardware device that he suggested people would carry in their pockets *in addition* to their cell phones. Then Neil got lots of his famous musician friends to endorse the system in hyper-exaggerated testimonials. The production plan looked solid, and his Kickstarter campaign raised many millions of dollars. How could he lose? And how could I win? I was nervous, jealous, and scared.

Turns out Pono, for all the money, fame, exposure, and social media, didn't get off the launchpad. But I had no way of knowing that would happen. I was terminally worried. I knew competition was a given in any entrepreneurial venture, and it's not always the best product that wins. As we know from politics, products, fashion, music, and movies, very often it's the team with the most money or the loudest message that wins the hearts and minds of voters and consumers. Time to worry some more.

Another comment on competition: Every market can handle more than a few suppliers. Just because you see competitors in your windshield (or rearview mirror), remember that most industries have many competitors. Think cars, TVs, medical devices, banks, fast food joints, consultancies, and so on. Don't let competition be the sole reason you ever give up.

Before diving headfirst into a possibly empty pool, we decided to do some consumer research. We connected one of our nineteen-inch pro rack products to a small headphone amp and plugged in an iPod and multiple pairs of headphones. We then asked anyone we could to tell us what their favorite music was, and we'd do a demo of a song they knew well. We'd play their music straight and then we'd hit the button on the Aphex processor. Every single time, their eyes would light up and their mouths would open wide as if to say, *Oh my god! That's amazing!*

It's not an exaggeration to explain Aphex processing could bring out detail to such a dramatic level that you could hear instruments that were otherwise buried in the combined lack of definition and overall distortion. Imagine hearing a song you know and love and being shocked to discover an additional guitar or singer. I'm serious. It's not that it wasn't there before, it just couldn't be heard. The signal was crushed, jumbled, mud. Or worse, it was only half the mud. Anyway, we did countless demos and confirmed that people loved what they were hearing.

It was the era of iPods and iPhones, and people were carrying their music collections with them at all times. It was incredible. They loved music. They invested in iTunes music files and streaming. They'd certainly spring a few dollars for something that could instantly make their entire music investment dramatically better. Right?

I thought so. I pushed our effort to the next phase: now to turn the hardware into software, then into an app. Two very different things. It took many months, but finally we had a working simulation of the hardware processor. Now we had to work it into an actual app. More design, more engineering, more consultants, more money . . .

We ended up hiring an impressive-sounding app development company based in California. They claimed all kinds of expertise, clients, and success—but they sucked. They wasted our time and money. This was getting expensive. We had to go on the hunt again. We ended up at a New York app development company. Big website. Lots of staff. Porsche as a client. I flew to New York and met with them. I brought one of my board members with me. I wanted some backup. Another view. Another opinion.

Their office was a swarm of millennials. It seemed like app heaven. We were led to a conference room. We sat down with a handful of youngsters and let them explain why we should work with them. The leader of the pack was a kid dressed in a T-shirt, corduroy jacket, and Moon Boots. I am not kidding. Moon Boots. In Manhattan. It wasn't even winter. I had trouble concentrating. Showing uncharacteristic control, I pushed back a bit. I told them they needed to come to Park City and *absorb* our ideas, plans, and culture. I needed them to understand that we were not total dinosaurs, that we had created lots of great products, technologies, marketing, and graphics. They needed to respect us to diffuse their arrogance, which was on high display.

More months, more money. But we got our app. I wanted to prove to the world that music could be enjoyed even more. Easily. Daily. Always. I contacted various artists that we'd worked with at Aphex to see if they'd help me expose our app to the world. One of the best pro demos I did was at Pat Metheny's home recording studio. Pat was a big Aphex user and an intense perfectionist when he was recording and performing. Heading to his place, I downloaded three of his cuts from iTunes. I wanted him to get a realistic demo. I already had lots of Pat's music on my iPod but as full-res files from CDs. I didn't want to give him the *best* demo, I wanted him to hear it the way modern-day fans were hearing his music: online purchased, low res and thin.

Pat put on headphones and pushed play. He toggled the Aphex processing button on and off, again and again. He was startled. He kept fiddling with the app's settings as he listened to multiple tracks. When he was done, he was both excited by how great the app was and shocked at how crummy the online purchased files were. These were the files his fans were buying. These were the tracks he'd painstakingly worked on in the recording studio to make perfect. It was the same with every other artist.

As for sales, that's another story. We had counted on the New York app experts' marketing team to advise us on the best strategy for sales. We had bounced all kinds of ideas around: free trials, free, charge, limited-time offers, basic and premium features, and so on. In the end, we offered the app for free for fifteen minutes a day to allow people unlimited demo days. If they wanted full-time use, they could pay five dollars or three dollars or—well, the price was a moving target and experiment.

The launch was painfully late. The New York company kept missing promised deadlines, though magically, their invoices were never late! Christmas season was in full swing. We launched. We had 300,000 downloads in just a few months, but people weren't converting to purchases. We weren't about to give up. We enlisted an energetic app sales company that had approached us. They appeared real, mature, and had their office in the Empire State Building—and no Moon Boots. Having been bitten, I signed and faxed over an agreement that only paid them commission for actual sales. There would be no advances, no retainers, no consulting fees. Sounded good. It wasn't.

One day, Julie, our Aphex keeper of records, books, and payroll, called to tell me she'd received an invoice for $125,000—commission for app sales. Odd, we hadn't seen any real sales yet. A few weeks later, she got a few calls asking for payment. And then badgering. Then threats of interest charges and other expenses. I jumped in and called our point person who assured me there was nothing to worry about. Then we received a letter from their attorney. It escalated from there. A bank called, claiming they were taking over the debt and that they'd prosecute.

Turns out they had their superstar lawyer insert an extra page into our already signed contract, totally revising their payment program before he faxed it back. What the idiot didn't do was trim the header off all the other pages of *my* fax he'd signed to hide the subterfuge. The page headers didn't match! What a crook! It was insane. They kept up the pressure tactics and hoped we'd fold and send them some big money. Out of frustration, we arranged a conference call with them, their lawyer, and their collection agent. We listened to their BS for a few minutes and then hit them with our ultimatum: Sue us! Please! We'd love it! Magically, that was the end of it. We never heard from them again. Oh yes, you guessed it…once again, I had to use creative genius to plot revenge.

Here's the (now obvious) lesson we learned during the app development project: digital products and business are really about user volumes and not about revenues (it was 2013, so this wasn't as obvious as you might think). What we should have done was give away the app for free. Totally free. No time limits and no tricks. Just give it away and get all those happy users to share it with their online friends. Damn, success was so close, but it got blown. Was it our inexperience or our costly New York consultants? Who cares? Blame gets old. The important thing is to be objective about why things fail.

After a lot of dollars and years of hard work, all I had to keep me from exploding was the knowledge that we'd created a superior technology and product that performed exactly as I had envisioned. There wasn't anything on the market like it, and everyone who used it—both consumers and professionals—loved it. They thought it was amazing. We had impressed a lot of people. I guess you have to take whatever you can from your efforts and celebrate the small victories, even while suffering the financial fails.

I wanted to advance technology and performance, style, and user experience—and no one cared. The sad reality is that people are incredibly shortsighted. They might invest hundreds, or thousands, on their music, but the idea of spending two or three measly dollars to vastly improve their entire collection is a nonstarter. Seems absurd, right? It is absurd, but it's real. The world had bitten hook, line, and sinker into the digital music revolution, and it really didn't care about sound quality. They just wanted convenience.

As the reality of day-to-day pro audio business torture came to a head, I knew there was just one solution. Sell, move on, and work on anything else. It was just too infuriating to fight an entrenched pattern of "good enough." I wasn't a creative entrepreneur just so I could be frustrated every day. I started hunting for a buyer. While almost nothing in the world of entrepreneurship ever happens quickly, I did get lucky, courtesy of a meeting with my friend Alan Parsons, to discuss more product and technology ideas. As we talked, I threw out a curveball. "What would you think if I told you what I really want is to sell the Aphex company? Any advice?" Alan shifted gears as smoothly as I worked a 911 gearbox. He didn't miss a beat. Alan, understanding my ongoing struggle, didn't fall back on my recent idea of an Alan Parsons signature line of Aphex products. Instead, he suggested I speak with Peter Freedman, owner of Røde microphones in Australia. Alan then made a two-sentence email introduction.

A few weeks later, I was flying to San Diego to be Peter's guest at a Røde event. We would have lunch and then talk business. We quickly sealed the deal. It took only an hour (maybe less) for us to lay out the details and numbers of a sale. Funny how he and I, as CEOs, figured out the details in such a short time, yet it took the lawyers six months to figure out how to put it on paper. No comment.

I realized too late that I'd made a huge mistake with Aphex. I allowed my excitement to cloud my judgment. There are always the if-onlys, and mine was this: if only I'd been smart enough to realize we didn't need to own Aphex. We should have simply stuck with licensing it. Instead, we dove in, and hard. I'd mortgaged our house, I'd brought in outside money, I'd slept about a third of what any healthy human should, and I suffered every possible business and emotional hit every week for five years. On top of all this, my family was stressed as they wondered if this venture was going to pay off—or pay at all. And they let me know it, with no shortage of complaints and demands, most of which just added more tension to my already full brain. I knew our company had amazing tech. The investors knew it too. We'd won lots of prestigious industry awards with our hardware and software. And this was a world of super technicians, engineers, producers, and artists. They knew what they were talking about. We just hit at the wrong time. The music world was changing and consumers didn't care.

Throwing more salt in my wounds, I'd sold off the great workshop we had in Utah, and that was a constant needle in my side. The hardest part of all was knowing that my investors lost money. I lost money. It was a hell ride, and I deserved it. A case of getting things wrong while having a lot of right puzzle pieces.

Failure is usually measured in financial terms. In this, we failed. But what is so often overlooked, forgotten, or diminished is the fact that we set a goal to create something that no one had ever done before. We not only achieved that goal but also created best-in-class technology that the most discerning experts in the industry endorsed as the best ever! That's no failure.

Attempting to balance out the torture I'd been through was the knowledge and experience of so many fun and exciting moments: I got to watch great artists work in studios, including Frank Zappa's historic studio (with his daughter serving us treats), and I drank a truckload of cocktails with all kinds of amazing musicians, producers, and sound engineers. I had a portfolio of memories—and friends. I always say I'm not an audiophile. It's true. I just love the music. I was a guitar player and performed at a very young age. I watched Cream, the Doors, the Turtles, Johnny, Pauly, the Dead, and so many others as a little kid and over the years. It tattooed me with a total devotion to rock and roll, and Aphex at least gave me a front-row ticket to the inner workings of rock.

After some months, the Aphex sale went through. We had created truly amazing products and technologies, and it was over. Then, like the old Rock 'Em Sock 'Em Robots toy, the serial entrepreneur just keeps getting back up after each knockout and marches into battle to do it again. That's our makeup. Our next project will be the big one. We are certain. More risk, more passion, more time, more stress. It's the drug that just keeps on giving. Next project, please!

CHAPTER 10

I NEED A SANITY OUTLET

HAVING PUT DWV WORK ON HOLD for several years to focus on the Aphex adventure had been hard, mostly because the daily creativity of DWV projects had been replaced by endless tech, management, investor relations, and other responsibilities, with only limited time for design and innovation. This wasn't part of my bigger plan, and all this added even more stress to an already high-stress career, not to mention my family life. It didn't help that after the sale of Aphex, I got talked into helping, and then running, a cybertechnology development project. What was I thinking?

I ended up as CEO, building a new company I named 7Tunnels, and we had a single goal: develop quantum-computer-resistant data encryption. This was never my idea, nor my area of expertise, but my eagerness to take on wild challenges had not dimmed, and I assembled a team of defense industry engineers and others as we took on this massive task.

While I was not the cybersecurity expert, I did have the other background experience to help guide this venture, and it wasn't long before we were asked by DuPont to create a custom version of our nascent technology to protect their executives as they sent communications to and from their fleet of DuPont jets. This would be our launchpad, or so we thought. We were advancing our technology. We were building a patent portfolio. All was going great with DuPont. They were paying us! We believed others would eventually follow. We were having meetings with the FBI, CIA, defense contractors, aviation and tech companies. Things felt promising, but funds were tight, so we needed a bit of luck. Then COVID-19 hit, sending all our engineers home as businesses everywhere went into a dive. Time to rethink how to commercialize or sell this powerful technology in a world that was shutting down. Argh!

I was extremely busy throughout the post-Aphex period, with the multi-year commitment to 7Tunnels and all it entailed, but I needed an outlet. Something for my creative side. Something to keep me sane and balanced. Thankfully, a few outlets found me—and DWV. The ensuing creative projects enhanced my 7Tunnels day job making me a happier and even more energized leader.

You can imagine how thrilled I was to be asked to design the livery and team image for a successful Porsche racing team that competed in the Pirelli World Challenge, a high-profile race series that attracted teams from Porsche, Ferrari, BMW, and others. The team's goal was not just to win but to make a statement doing it. Knowing their car was the crown jewel of their image, I started there and designed five options to cover their car. As a former racer and motorsports participant at various levels, I wanted to leverage my knowledge of racing marketing to do something that hadn't been done before. I created a design that had camera magnetism. Something compelling to anyone and everyone at the track. Something completely different and something that would stand out from the crowd, as I like to say. I created the Peacemobile. It would be so unexpected and so graphic. Imagine one of the most revered racing cars of all time covered from one end to the other with a kaleidoscope of colorful peace symbols—almost the antithesis of horsepower, noise, speed, and power, yet so universal and important a message, conveyed in a most unique setting.

The other four proposed designs were good and interesting. One even spoke to the business of the primary sponsor, with digital images of tools and hardware bits to promote their construction industry software product. Thankfully, the team owner loved the Peacemobile concept. Unfortunately, the secondary sponsor, a mortgage company, wasn't quite so forward-thinking, and worse, their director of marketing fancied himself quite the motorsports expert. To him, the Peacemobile was too "out there." What he didn't consider was that this car would be photographed more than any other car in the series, and that meant their logos would be as well. And therein lies the rub of doing contract work: you can be visionary, creative, and truly knowledgeable about your subject and still get crushed by the client, or in this case, the client's sponsor. It happens all the time. Be prepared and decide whether to hold your tongue or let it fly. I've done both. I prefer the latter.

On the positive side, they chose my least favorite, but it was still a standout on the track, in the pits, and in the paddock. The racing team's owner, Steve Urry, was the kind of guy who spared no expense to do a first-class job. He understood the benefits of standing out from the crowd (he loved the Peacemobile), and he brought that impressive attitude and approach to racing. On everything from driver uniforms to semitruck transporters and everything in between, the designs DWV created made a statement of professionalism and quality. I was proud of the work we did for the team, and in the end, it was a success all around. The team racked up victories, and Steve totally raised the bar on image, performance, and style in the Pirelli series.

In a loosely related adventure, *000 Magazine* is the result of a total commitment by two car magazine industry veterans to create "A quarterly art journal that just happens to be about Porsche." Pete Stout and Alex Palevsky were fulfilling a design and entrepreneurial dream that I was introduced into by Michael Jordan, the art director of *Porsche Panorama* magazine. It turned out to be a good match, as my product design, art, and writing helped them further change people's impressions of what a car magazine could be. They commissioned a custom David Wiener signature desk accessory of milled aluminum and machine screws that harkened back to details on early 911s and Porsche race cars. Naturally, I was thrilled by Pete and Alex's drive, passion, and quest for the best. As Pete says, they strive to make *000* attractive to people who don't even care about cars. DWV designed and produced hundreds of these elegant pieces that embodied the essence of my design and automotive thinking.

A while later, I was approached with another classic DWV doozie: design a new petroleum cleaning and processing plant. Of course, I had no knowledge of these technologies, but with guidance from the scientists and engineers who had created a truly innovative process that would one day transform this industry, I set about creating a new kind of processing plant that would be beautiful to look at while performing exactly as needed. Industrial sculpture or architecture? When it's built, you can decide. I can't wait.

And speaking of sculpture, I got a chance during all the solitary of COVID to present my proposal for a major public outdoor sculpture to be the centerpiece of the Pendry Hotel and Canyons Resort's village makeover. With a national field of over one hundred artists presenting, they selected my proposal, and again I was thrust into doing something I'd never done before. Thankfully, my close friend and artist Greg Ragland introduced me to an amazing foundry, and that team held my hand as I produced the engineering drawings and CAD files (with the very convenient help of my DWV team) and then did hands-on fabrication and installation oversight of the twenty-foot-tall stainless steel monster. I learned a lot and couldn't believe all the red tape around county and building codes, from electrical and earthquake safety to fire codes and emergency vehicle access and more! This was no minor project or process, but the end result was spectacular, and everyone involved was thrilled with the sculpture, *Grand Prix*.

Here's another. In my never-ending quest for creative design and innovation, the Golden Bolt was a true escapist venture into the world of spinner toys. I needed to do something fun and a bit funny to maintain my sanity during the intensely serious cybersecurity work of 7 Tunnels, so I created the ultimate desk accessory: a twenty-four-karat-gold-plated industrial nut and bolt that you could play with while on phone calls at your desk. When I say *industrial*, I mean one full pound of golden beauty. To help launch this idea, I created a video with my son Weston and asked my friend Alan Parsons to provide the voice-over. It was a total send-up. I did improv as Weston filmed and then cut together a great piece. The Golden Bolt was not meant to be a major business endeavor; it was more of a creative outlet and cool gift idea. Little investment. Lots of fun. People loved it. Sundance Film Festival bought a lot for their VIPs. As

Alan says in the video after listing a long string of DWV products and accomplishments, "And now, finally, it's all led to this!"

Maintain a sense of humor and don't take yourself too seriously! As I often say, "I take my work seriously, but I don't take myself seriously." Try it.

There have been a lot more projects, products, ideas, artwork, and adventures over the years. I haven't slowed down, and I don't plan to. In recent years, we've been deep into design for race cars, luxury clothing, and other things, while still working on our 7 Tunnels mission. I've been creating more artwork and had a number of international art exhibits. I keep massaging my associations with Formula One, America's Cup sailing, and World Cup skiing for some projects in the works, and there are other things that will play a role in new DWV programs. And through my automotive artwork, I've been connected with another exciting and amazing automotive magazine. The Road Rat in London has taken an artistic approach to the world of automotive journals, and I am happy to be adding them to my list of DWV projects.

So I have managed to find creative outlets while grinding away with my team at developing the most powerful data encryption technology we are aware of. Like the Aphex app, this is a technology that is a total game-changer, but unlike our music app, it is important to the country, the population and the security of America. We continue to work to put this in the hands of the right people who know what to do with it. Stay tuned.

Forty years on, I've worked with so many great people, as well as a few terrible ones, and created countless stories. Many more than could ever be told here. It's been a wild ride and it's not even over.

Where does all this leave us? Time for some reflection.

CHAPTER 11

THE PAINT NEVER DRIES

NO MATTER HOW MUCH I WORK or how much I've done, it's never enough. It's never satisfying. It's just another "project," as I refer to everything I do. There's no end in sight. The good news is I love what I do. The bad news is I'm not going to slow down. I want to figure out how to execute my idea for a ride-smoothing system for small boats. I want to see WindTunnel clothing on the shelves. I want to build my idea for a custom Porsche 911 that's been marinating for years. I also want to find time for more adventures with Kate and my family.

It's insane, but I get bored a lot. Not bored as in sitting on the couch with nothing to do. Bored as in I achieve something I set out to do, and when I've done it, I need to attempt something new. Often the new thing is something I know nothing about or didn't ever plan. That's the accidental madness of all this. I used to joke that about the time my work got on a magazine cover, I'd quit that industry. Jumping around from hardware to clothing to electronics to vehicles to furniture and back again has always been about wanting to create versus getting mired in day-to-day minutia or worrying about how many #8 screws we had in stock.

But the reality is you need to know how to do something to do it right. It would have been easy to believe my college advisor, Herb Bernstein, about "You don't really need to worry about all the fine engineering details." I didn't buy it. I always believed I needed to understand the details of *how*, even if I couldn't always explain the *why*. I had to get my hands dirty so I could design and engineer better, more efficient machines; sew clothing so I could understand how fabrics fit and move; and design app interfaces to improve human interaction with technology. I had to understand metals, composites, plastics, circuits, electronics, vehicle dynamics, hardware, soft-goods production, and so much more. This knowledge helped me improve material usage, yields, and margins while always pushing quality and performance as the number one goal. Later, I had to understand marketing, sales, graphics, digital production, and more so I could create—and produce—seamless and integrated offerings. And then came the web, and social media (which I am still learning).

Speaking of learning, here are some things I learned along my journey that might provide ideas or inspiration for your adventures. Grab what makes sense and toss the rest. After all, by now you may just think I'm a nut job.

I learned that knowledge meant nothing without good, solid people behind you. Corporate culture is defined by the attitude of those within a company. How leadership and employees think, feel, and act reflects the company's values. Imagine working in a company where you hate the culture. Miserable, right? That's why the culture of DWV did not happen by accident. It is perhaps the one thing that I have consciously focused on to ensure it accurately reflects my values. There are five leading principles we strive to maintain:

- *Beyond Ideas*. Prioritize creativity *and* execution.
- *The Fountainhead*. Understand the mechanics of what must be done. It's not just pretty pictures.
- *Differentiation*. Never be a copycat player.
- *Timelessness*. Make things that last and never lack in performance or style. Trendy sucks.
- *Formula One Culture*. Operate at the highest level possible within your means at all times.

As you know, my passion for Formula One and racing began as a little kid. I've always felt a special connection to the sport, and that drove me to choose performance and style as hallmarks of my work. I've used Formula One as a basis for inspiring and guiding my teams in various businesses, homing in on the idea that having total commitment and a desire to achieve specific goals is the only way to truly succeed. It's not trite. Realizing that even the most seemingly insignificant mistake can have a major negative impact is a serious form of daily thinking. People think a 1 percent product failure rate is good. It's not. That's one person in one hundred who's left dissatisfied, and that's not winning.

When we manufacture various products, I set up critical quality control, testing, fit, and finish programs for our teams to ensure no failed product leaves our shop. This was never more crucial than when we partnered with Ferrari on the elegant and hugely expensive Art.Engine home audio system. We were shipping a 110-pound piece of custom-built, gleaming audio gear all over the globe, and the owners were not likely to tolerate a mistake, be it a scratch or a nonfunctioning device—and I wouldn't tolerate paying to ship it back and forth! We weren't just selling a sound system—we were selling awe itself. We had to be perfect.

Talking about team members, here's one nobody talks about: your gut. When you head to your office, be sure to take your gut to work. Trust your gut. I mean it. Most people get feedback from their gut but often ignore it, especially when the feedback is troubling. It's much easier to talk yourself out of the troubling issue than deal with the problem employee, customer, attorney, accountant, or whatever. I have talked myself out of believing my gut many times. In the early days, it usually involved problem employees I believed were critical to the team, those I was afraid we couldn't survive without despite knowing the frustration, worry, and nightmare lying ahead. Did I listen to my gut? Nah. And I paid for it.

Understand that the business world is populated with no shortage of individuals who are more focused on their own greed and self-importance than they are on being honest and productive. They will grab your money, claim they are the reason for anything good, and run for the hills to avoid having to deal with anything bad. They will lie, cheat, steal, torture you, and waste your time. I have seen it so many times it's insane. I've heard individuals in assorted ventures try to take credit for everything while having done nothing. Truly tiring, especially when you are 100 percent committed, putting in time—and your own money—while they put in nothing. They want advanced pay, loans, stock, and more while providing nothing of real value. Beware. These are expensive lessons, and your gut is almost always right. Be smart. Be brave. Listen to your gut!

Lucky for me—and for most entrepreneurs—there are great people hidden among the energy vampires. The great ones don't lead off with what's in it for them. They don't try to impress. They speak in normal voices and typically have inspiring and intelligent things to say. The key is to find as many of these people as you can. Make friends with them. Bring them into your adventures. Put them on your advisory boards. Just hang out. Listen and learn.

Moving on, the thing most people never really understand is risk. For an entrepreneur, risk is the one constant. Will I be successful? Will I build something meaningful? Will I be able to pay my team? Will I make any money? Will my spouse kill me? What if I fail? Accountants, lawyers, burger flippers, and so many other traditionally employed people don't have these same risks. Sure, they all worry about money—everyone does—and they worry about their kids, their families, their job security, and such, but they don't typically have to worry about making payroll, signing office leases, product liability, rivets, bolts, zippers, and the million other things that people who create and grow businesses do. Some people are cut out for risk in business, and some just aren't. There's no right or wrong, good or bad, smart or dumb. It's just a matter of what road you decide to take. I didn't become an entrepreneur just to make big bucks. It was about so much more, and I've always been willing to risk everything in my chase to create and achieve.

So where is the balance? How do you take that entrepreneurial leap of faith and not plunge to the ground? The chicken-and-egg question comes to mind: Do you make money, then take the leap, or do you take the leap and make the money? It's impossible to know, but one thing is certain: if you are truly committed, you can find ways to survive. I don't mean *you can do anything you set your mind to*. That's one of those throwaway parenting lines. No, I am talking true commitment. But what does that look like, and how will you know if you have it?

As they say, there is no magic, so you can't just will it to happen like a Jedi mind trick. You can make intelligent plans and find ways to get to your goals, even if it means more work and slow progress. I learned this early on when I decided, even before I had my driver's license, that I was going to drive a Porsche. I was committed to this dream but had no money, so I took on every paying job I could get or force my way into. I didn't care what the job was as long as I could ride my bike to the bank and deposit some small amount of money in my interest-bearing savings account. Miracle of all miracles, by the end of eleventh grade, I was driving the car of my dreams, and no one could convince me that the old car I had rebuilt was anything less than amazing. Remember, real passion is a powerful business tool.

So you now have your company set up and going, and maybe you have a partner or employees. Maybe you are close to success. Or maybe you are close to circling the bowl. Sometimes success is a knife's edge away and you just need another injection of cash. Success is a very misunderstood aspect of creativity and entrepreneurship. How do you define success? Is success all about money? Most people measure themselves with money. I love money, but I view it as fuel. For example, I have always been committed to nice cars, and I always will have material dreams, but I temper this with the knowledge that I will gladly sell any of it if I need the money for a business venture. More than once I've sold off a dream car, guitar, or piece of art in order to pay bills or order more inventory. Do I regret it? Not at all. I treat it as my internal badge of courage. My measurement of success: my own admission that my work and dreams are more important than any material item or bank statement.

Remember: success is about achieving your dreams. That's it. For me, it's creating an amazing innovation, designing a popular product, hitting a sales goal, and doing something special for my team, my family, and myself. Whatever your dream is, make it happen.

Sometimes success can sneak up on you. When it does, celebrate it. Enjoy it. It will be fleeting if you are really pushing yourself. Some years after I sold my SoundTube shares, I was at Ferrari in Maranello, shooting photos for future artwork. On a visit to the Enzo Ferrari Museum in Modena, the lights dimmed, and a movie about Enzo suddenly filled the huge space. When it ended, I looked up and noticed that all the speakers were SoundTubes! I was full circle, and it felt good to know Ferrari had selected my speakers for their premier museum. Celebrate, then move along. And remember, many of your successes may not get proper attention from others, so be your own cheerleader. Then move along.

I've had dozens of ventures and projects over the past forty years—many exciting, only a few less than that. I've made people a lot of money and lost money for others. Many of my creations can be seen around the world every day, while a few have fizzled. One thing I can say with total confidence is that every product, vehicle, fashion line, brand, and technology was best-in-class when it was introduced to the market, and that is a great achievement. A great career. People take this for granted or don't even consider it. As I said earlier, most people only focus on money as a measure.

For me, the goal has always centered on creativity and innovation. True innovation. Advancing the state of the art. While others are happy to copy or never take the chance, my career has been about daring to do the things people told me were impossible. Or crazy.

My successes—the way I always measured them—have been about whether they have pushed the boundaries. Whether they were better than whatever else was available. Whether there *was* anything available. I always hoped they would make money. Lots of money. But that wasn't the point. Never. The point was always to be the best. The first. The innovator. And if no one noticed, that didn't stop me.

So where does it end? Or does it end? After I sold my first company, friends asked Kate if I was going to retire. She said, "Yes, for a day." I think that sums it up. This life and drive never end. If you love what you do and you've got more than one trick, you don't think about retiring. You think about the next idea, the next venture, the next challenge, and if you've got just a wee bit of a competitive nature, you want to see if your next thing will be bigger, better, and badder than all the previous experiments. It's like saltwater fly fishing: every fish is exciting, but you don't dwell on the fish of the past. You are always thinking about the next one.

I said I'd never retire. There are too many projects I still want to do. But there are always the dream projects that you think may never actually happen. Well, dreams do come true. Sort of. Recently, out of nowhere, I was introduced to people in the fashion business who had heard about the WindTunnel luxe clothing concept I'd been outlining for years. They loved it, and after months of meetings, they told me they wanted to back the project, pay me a ton, and leave me in control of the whole thing. This was truly a dream project—a dream opportunity. And best of all, WindTunnel featured Formula One motorsports, America's Cup yacht racing, and World Cup skiing as themes for the clothing. Of course there's always a bump in the road. After a year of big money, the backers lost their funding, which meant WindTunnel lost its funding. And once again, the entrepreneur must be bullet-proof in order to take the punches and keep on fighting. These things happen. You can't predict them. You just get back up and go again. Who knows, maybe new backers will drop in from heaven.

What is the future of entrepreneurship and creativity in business? If you look at the impact that crowdfunding has had on helping people launch their ideas, you quickly realize that the job of entrepreneur or creative has radically changed over the past ten or fifteen years. Now almost anyone with *any* level of passion or commitment can test the waters. Long ago, market testing happened by actually making something, setting up a table or display, and putting on a product performance to see if anyone cared or would commit to buying what you were offering. Today, you can do it all from the comfort of your bedroom. The timeframe from initial concept to market validation has been shrunk, streamlined, and fine-tuned in such a way that you can hit your target audience, target dealers, and target media very quickly, and they eat it up.

It's easier than ever to test-drive your ideas before you invest a ton of time, money, and blood into it, but remember: if you commit to a digital funding campaign and you get funded, you have to deliver. That means you have to become a manufacturer *and* a sales force *and* a customer service operation—*and, and, and*. Even if you outsource your production to a contract manufacturer that makes your product and ships you cases of them, you are still the manufacturer. You must perform. You are responsible. You are liable. What if your product fails, injures someone, kills someone, or burns down a house? Think it through. Apply common sense. All of these issues can be overcome with time, energy, talent, and money, but it's critical to temper your enthusiasm with a businessperson's sensibilities when you dive into your online dream. Creativity leads. Responsibility follows.

As we approach the end of this story, I want to highlight a few of the great people I have been lucky enough to turn into friends and business associates over the many years and crazy adventures that have punctuated my career. Each is an overachiever, a driven soul, and a leader in their industry and community. You've already read about them in brief, but each is worthy of more detail because they have been so inspirational to me along my journey.

JEAN TODT

I met Jean Todt when I was working to partner with Ferrari to create a high-visibility statement product, and Jean was their CEO. Before being appointed CEO, Jean was the mastermind behind the winningest era in Ferrari Formula One history. Jean was brought in to turn around the F1 team and quickly applied his absolute performance mindset to gutting and reengineering the culture of the most famous team in motorsports. It was Jean who provided Michael Schumacher with cars, equipment, strategy, and consistency to take Michael to his record seven World Championships. Jean's talents and achievements were all the more amazing because he was a Frenchman brought in to lead this legendary Italian team. This was shocking to many in the religion of Ferrari, but he totally showed them. Not an Italian. Not a Catholic. A former rally-racing pro turned creator of a dream team and god of the *Tifosi*.

I saw this firsthand while walking through the Modena airport with him and witnessing the behavior all around us. It was Jean's miracle turnaround of the F1 team that led the board to appoint him CEO of the entire company while also the director of the F1 team. When his tenure at Ferrari was coming to a close, Jean didn't step down and rest on his laurels: he was voted president of the Fédération Internationale de l'Automobile, the governing body of all motorsports worldwide.

This is a man who didn't understand failure, yet he was prone to eating his fingernails as he battled to achieve the next win. He has always been inspiring, and all the more so when I was invited to his country home outside Paris. What impressed me the most was my time wandering around his office above his massive barn garage. It wasn't all the photos of Jean with a staggering list of famous drivers and personalities. It wasn't the extraordinary collection of famous motorsports memorabilia. And it wasn't his collection of beautiful black Ferraris in the garage below. What impressed me were the notes to himself posted around the room as reminders to ensure he performed at his best. Jean was a gentleman and honest person every time we were together. In his home, his apartment, his plane, his office. He's impressive at a level that's hard to believe, and it's his hard work and poise that have made Jean Todt the racer, manager, director, leader, businessperson, politician, advisor, admirer of the arts, host, and modest human that he is.

PETER METCALF

I met Peter through a board member of mine who figured Peter and I would have a lot in common. He was a world-class rock climber, *Guinness Book* athlete, successful entrepreneur, naturalist, and poster boy for the outdoor industry and open lands. Lucky for me, when we met at Black Diamond, the company he founded out of Patagonia clothing, Peter was gracious and keyed in on my interest in performance design and manufacturing. He then gave me a tour of their facilities and factory. I was enthralled by the company's labyrinth of underground manufacturing shops, rooms, and assembly and test labs.

Even after twenty-nine years of developing a tight-knit friendship with Peter, I am never surprised by my ongoing admiration for his knowledge, talent, drive, and commitment. He applies this to everything he does, from sport to food to travel to preserving the outdoors. In our early years, Peter played the roles of advisor, director, and friend, seeing me through the creation, development, and sale of multiple companies and ventures. Along the way, we always found time to squeeze in dinners to catch up on all the things we wanted to talk about that were unrelated to business. Even today, we typically spend three hours per dinner and share endless stories, ideas, personal details, and dreams, yet we always leave feeling like we haven't even scratched the surface. Clearly we need a lot more dinners.

I am always impressed by Peter's subtle references to history, books, authors, and experts. His dialogue is peppered with poignant quotes and words like *criminal*, *brutal*, *anachronism*, and *sublime* that help make powerful points. Talking with him is always educational, inspiring, and above all else, fun, but what separates Peter from so many others is his total commitment to being just and fair, honest and ethical. These are characteristics that stand out so strongly that it's hard to believe anyone would ever argue his points, whether in his Capitol Hill testimony on the environment or in a conversation among his industry peers. Understated power is how I think of Peter.

ALAN PARSONS

I hold few people in high esteem from my days in the audio industry, but Alan Parsons is chief among them. Not just a legendary artist and producer, he is an incredibly modest superstar. I was introduced to Alan during my Aphex days, and he was an early endorser of Aphex gear and continued his use and appreciation of our products long after his original deal was done.

As a guitar-rocking teenager in the '70s, I knew of the Alan Parsons Project but never focused on the group or its music. Fast-forward to

2010, and we became instant friends, sharing drinks and laughs while sitting with Alan's wife, Lisa, and a few characters from the music world. I immediately went out and bought all the Alan Parsons and Alan Parsons Project CDs I could find. I wanted to know his music. I put the first CD on and was surprised as songs I recognized kept popping up. These were songs I loved but had never taken the time in high school to learn who the artist was. This continued as I played through seven or eight CDs. I was amazed. I had no idea that Alan had so many hits and songs that were being used globally for a variety of programs and commercials. I felt like a music neophyte, and I was embarrassed. This man was truly a legend, and he was still creating music decades later. I felt honored to get so much time with him.

Over the next few years, Alan became a trusted voice and sounding board for me. Never once did he ask for anything. No gear. No money. Nothing. Unlike so many other musicians and producers, Alan didn't see me as another audio manufacturer gear-grab opportunity. It just wasn't part of his equation. He was simply an honest and true talent, and he never once acted like he was someone special. And for that reason, I happily gave him gear to use, test, and critique.

When I proposed that Alan should make an appearance at our next NAMM show—the biggest music and rock trade show of the year—he was all about helping me promote Aphex to the masses of musicians, industry people, and fans. Alan sat through a staggering line of people that ran laps around our show booth, down the aisle, and around the corner at the far end of the Anaheim Convention Center—and these characters came prepared. They'd seen our promo posters announcing Alan's appearance, and they brought albums, T-shirts, posters, skin, and more for Alan to sign. He was a gentleman throughout and tolerated every personal story, every "I'm your biggest fan," and other bits of fan insanity. It was just one more display of Alan's modesty, generosity, and respect for those around him. It's hard to imagine all this from someone who cut his engineering teeth on a London rooftop with the Beatles and was called the fifth member of Pink Floyd for his work on *Dark Side of the Moon* (only the most popular album of all time), not to mention his endless hit parade.

Alan was a star when it was time for me to try to sell the Aphex company. His advice and help were instrumental in me closing a deal, yet to Alan, it was nothing more than a simple email. Never once did he have his hand out asking for anything. Even more reason for me to send a collection of wines and a check as a simple thank you.

ERIC HEIDEN

I met Eric when I was creating the land speed record bike for my college thesis. A chance phone call to his house resulted in a forty-year friendship and some wild adventures. The impact and inspiration that has come from being around Eric is what strikes the biggest chord for me. Here's a guy who won all five gold medals for speed skating in one Olympics, then he turns down endless endorsement deals because he's not in it for the money or fame. That's Eric. Instead, he decides he wants to race bikes and make it to the Tour de France, which he does as the leader of the 7-Eleven cycling team, the first American team to enter and then win stages, all while studying at Stanford to become an orthopedic surgeon! He later became a celebrated surgeon to a long list of Olympic athletes and "regular" people.

I remember phoning him while he was in medical school and always being amazed, thinking he was probably sitting in a lab room surrounded by books, working his tail off—one of the most celebrated athletes in history. Eric is modest, soft-spoken, and always fun to be with. He talks to me like my work and achievements are more important than his own, which couldn't be further from the truth. It's this kind of behavior and character that drives me to work harder and take more chances. Eric and his family moved to Park City some years back, providing a great opportunity for us to continue to get together for fun, drinks, and appointments to decipher my various sporting injuries. Lucky me! When we get together with his other friends in town, it seems like Kate and I are the only two in the group who aren't Olympians or gold medalists. That says something about the company you keep. But it's always a great time and I always learn something new.

MY MOM

Honest. Thoughtful. Caring. Never focused on herself. It's 2001, and I turn on late-night TV in my Florida hotel room. There's a Martha Stewart documentary on, with a parade of people slamming Martha with assorted petty, and not-so-petty, gripes and snipes. Who didn't slam Martha? My mom was the only person. Mom said positive things about Martha. My mom worked with Martha—before she was *Martha*—in the two-person fine food boutique of the Common Market in Westport. Our families were friends, and through all of Martha's future challenges, my mom was steady, unmoved by gossip and public opinion.

Mom was, without question, my biggest fan, even when she had no idea what I was talking about or doing. She just believed. Of course, it wasn't totally blind support—she worked for Hermes for twenty years *after* a string of jobs at other luxury fashion brands, like Bergdorf Goodman, Bottega Veneta, and Henri Bendel. Mom knew her stuff and just wanted to see me succeed. We hear talk of unconditional love, but it's really something when we experience it for ourselves. We entrepreneurs sure need it! The phone calls I had with her up until she was ninety-two were fun, intelligent, and thought-provoking. She always had questions and ideas that were different and interesting. She made the world more interesting. The people she worked with tell me that every time I visit them. My friends tell me that. I experienced that. She was great.

FINAL THOUGHTS

As the world of business and entrepreneurship evolves, some things will never change. The common denominators will always be creativity, risk, funding, personnel, follow-through, performance, and customer service. With this in mind, you have to chase your dreams. As Phil Knight of Nike fame said in his book, *Shoe Dog*:

Do not settle for a job or a profession or even a career. Seek a calling. Even if you don't know what that means, seek it. If you're following your calling, the fatigue will be easier to bear, the disappointments will be fuel, the highs will be like nothing you've ever felt.

It's so true. The elation I felt—and feel—every time we pack up a product to ship out or see one of my designs in a magazine or on exhibit instantly wipes away all my built-up stress and frustration. I know this from so many years and experiences that I no longer let the stress crush me the way it used to. I know that the act of being creative can override the long hours, days, and weeks of suffering through the hard work and struggle. I know that the joy of seeing others get that wow out of something I have conjured can instantly cure all prior troubles. And if the money follows, even better. Of course, you know where that will go: right into the next project.

Half my reason for writing this book was that I was sick of hearing and reading so many so-called experts spouting off their advice: *The Ten Critical Pieces for Success, The Top Ten Things You Need to Be an Entrepreneur,* and worst of all, *How to Make a Million Dollars.* Forget it! Get real. Practice the dying art of common sense, then chase your dreams—hard!

Remember this: you measure yourself by the people who measure themselves by you.

THANK YOU

I'D LIKE TO THANK the following people for making this book and my adventures possible. Just remember that in a career spanning forty years, there's just no way I can remember to mention everyone. I hope they will forgive me.

First and foremost, to my wife and children: Kate, Weston, Hans, and Enzo. You now know them. Best thing about them is that we all love being together anytime we can make it happen. It's always fun, exciting, active and adventurous. More great times ahead. You are the best!

My very good friend of twenty-five years and my right arm at DWV, Francesca Thompson—thank you for all the hard work on so many varied ventures, for helping me with this book, and for your endless support, demanding behavior, and great humor.

My mother, Eva Wiener, an amazing person with an amazing life story. Even at ninety-two years old, she was going hard all the way to the end. We had a lot of fun. My mom was the definition of unconditional support. I really miss our daily calls that covered a wild spectrum of topics. My Mutti!

And a special thank you to the people who have invested in my work over the years—those who made a lot of money and particularly those who did not. You know that it wasn't for a lack of effort and belief.

And to the legions of people who have had an impact, made me laugh, love, smile, risk, test, and push the limits over so many years. This is a long list and I realize it's not what you typically find at the end of a book, but I want to acknowledge these people who were, and are, so important to me: *Life* photographer and my earliest mentor, George Silk; my first and truly amazing DWV assistant, Sharon McClaskie; engineering legend Paul MacCready (RIP); Tom Feeley; my great friend at Hampshire and early investment risk-taking guide, Matt Balk; former Ferrari CEO and FIA president, inspiration, and friend, Jean Todt; my two sidekicks in shooting, hunting, skinning and charring meats, and most importantly, co-piloting the Cruel Car, Ken Levin and Dave McHugh (RIP); Hampshire advisors and famed professors extraordinaire, Herb Bernstein and Ray Coppinger (RIP); music industry friend and my personal guide at the Grammys, Robbie Clyne; my legendary architect grandfather, Samuel G. Wiener (see the documentary!); my maternal grandmother, Bella Michel, who was the single toughest person I've ever known, told stories of escaping the Nazis, and laughed with me as her heart gave out; Olympic legend, my world speed record test pilot, and good friend, Eric Heiden; one of the first Aphex users and a lifelong inspiration, Paul McCartney; my guide along the guitar path, Eric Clapton; my best friend in boating, skiing, and general youthful mischief, Scott Reichhelm, and the third leg of our danger crew, Robert Davidson (RIP); race driver, playboy, and my earliest Ferrari employer, Coco Chinetti; my brothers-in-law and brothers-in-arms, Andy and Hank Ashforth; Flarecraft founder and longtime supporter, Bill Russell;

investor, supporter, creator of two of our amazing homes, and my Park City brother, Steve Urry; music legend Alan Parsons and his lovely wife, Lisa, who have been amazing to me for so many years; my two world champion whitewater kayaking girlfriends who pushed me early on to be better, Cathy Hearn and Kathy Sisk Tucker; my great Aphex board member and cousin-in-law, Eric Spomer; my mom's partner in selling fine foods before fine foods were a thing, family friend, inspiration, and provider of my first bartending job, Martha Stewart; the team at Ferrari in Maranello who bought into my wild and ambitious ideas; provider of my first fashion job, speed skier and skiwear legend, C. B. Vaughn; family friend since Scott and I were young and mentor to me for so many decades, George Reichhelm; Bob Wheaton; amazing Westport friend and provider of my NYC office at a moment's notice, Bob "Whoa Bobby" Corroon; the fifty people of SoundTube Entertainment back in the good old days; racing impresario and supplier of not one but two different Ferrari race cars for me to emblazon with SoundTube graphics, Gerry Jackson; Mr. Amazing—Bobby Foster; Susie Nielsen; Mark McHugh; Francois Sicard; Joel Roos; the legend of climbing, Black Diamond, and superfriend, Peter Metcalf; my separated-at-birth twin and cousin, Jimmy Weiss, and his (our) more-than-amazing parents, Marion and Don (RIP); Rob Barrett; my friend and regular sounding board, Dave Wilson; David Harries; Peter Freedman; two of my favorite DWV team members and managers of my time and budgets, Susan Richter and Hillary Howard; 7Tunnels geniuses Mike Adams and Mike Hammon (RIP); my two Connecticut patent gurus for decades, David Gordon and David Jacobson; Sean Forsgren; DWV digital master, Mikhail Nosikov; US Ski Team and now US Speedskating president, Ted Morris; Westport friend and the man who pushed me over the hump and into collector car dreams, Dick Ward; my Utah 7Tunnels patent master, Greg Baker; my occasionally supportive and always critical father, Sam Wiener (RIP); 7Tunnels board members and advisors, John Averill, Fuzzy Furr, Landel Hobbs, Chuck House, Tom Faust and Ken Campbell; DuPont's aviation tech wizard, committed friend, and brother in my mission to educate the encryption world, Brad Townsend (RIP); always amazing 7Tunnels attorney and advisor, Tom Talley; artiste and cohort in telemark skiing, Masters swimming, and other sketchy athletic ideas, Greg Ragland; friend and 7Tunnels believer, Dan Gelston; friend and book-writing inspiration, George Petersen a.k.a. Jack Carr; friend since kindergarten and partner in too many crimes that helped forge the path, Chris Sawch, and our Westport crew that maintains our close ties with too much fun, food, and drink, John Magruder, Rich Eldh, Ray Forehand, Danny Bennewitz, Jon Filderman, and Mike Westcott (RIP); my Masters stars who work me over in the pool, Leif Oines (who also provided advice on this book), Cindy Carmack, and Jim Lawrence; my Westport realtor and friend who taught me "pigs get fed and hogs get slaughtered," which has served me well in business and in life, Chari Polley; Former CBS News host Bill Kurtis for giving me my first network TV time—and saving me as I froze for the first fifteen seconds; rocking musician who treated me like I was more impressive than he was, John Paine of Asia; Ben Cohen for hiring DWV very early in my career to help make the ice cream even better; racing legend David Hobbs for being our personal handler as Kate and I celebrated part of our honeymoon at the German Grand Prix, giving Kate the most inside view possible of Formula One and introducing her to Alain Prost and Ayrton Senna; drummer Dan "Danski" Wojciechowski and his band's leader, the incomparable Peter Frampton, who were both so generous to me and my family; the team that trains me to calm down and shoot straight, Kurtis Hill, Henry Hudson, and Lars Magnusson; Howard Rubin of Kombi fame; creative force and SoundTube friend, Peter Gabriel; legendary Brumos Porsche racer Peter Gregg, who treated me and my racing dreams with honor (RIP); Pat Metheny, who graciously agreed to test the Aphex app and loved it as we sat in his home studio playing music; Cem Boyner of Beyman in Turkey; supporters of my work Apolo Ohno, Jonny Lang, Skunk Baxter, Joey Molland, Elan Morrison, Bela Fleck, Vic Wooten, Dan Levitan, Chip Ganassi, and Peter Bourassa; family friend, renowned tensegrity sculptor, and inspiration to me, Ken Snelson (RIP); Robby Ross; Mel Lavitt and Colin Hull; Leon Heyward and Bobby "Fish" James; "Billy Bob" Kiedaisch; Sean Doyle; Steve Taylor; my Florence gallery stars, Vito Abba and Carlotta Marzaioli; my Hampshire brother, Matt "Reltney" Polstein; supporter and the person always ready with answers to my emails, McLaren F1's Zak Brown; Steve Gorski; Diana Hart; Ford and GM legend and provider of advice, John Devine; Jerry Ward (RIP); the king of tennis, Pheasant Hill, and Istanbul, Don Galliers; dirty little fun-haver and friend since first grade, Scotty Morehouse; guitar supplier to the stars – and me, Dan Armstrong; friend and book-writing advisor, Carole Reichhelm; Porsche Panorama editor and supporter, Michael Jordan; Mark Maziarz; Steve Surprise (RIP); friend, saltwater guide and on-water counselor, Dan Marini; *Cars Yeah* podcast host and the real TurboMan, Mark Greene; John Cuccio (RIP)—*Forza, Mr. Cuccio!* Amazing printer of so much DWV paper, Danny Oblad and his crew; keepers of the fish and providers of my calming place on Andros Island, Liz and Alton Bain; for his endless enthusiasm and tolerance, Noah Flood; foundry magicians, Kevin and the team at Metal Arts; journo Kirsten Nelson; Connan Ashforth for always being there for me—you're the best! SRS's Mike and Matt; Brandon Scott; design publisher Susen Sawatzki; Sean Harris at Ferrari SLC; David Borish; Tom "T-Money" Gorton for so many things; Blaine Parker; Chris Combest; Gary Liden; Julie Garcia; Raymond Lui; Hendrik Huebscher; Mike Denny; Francie, for helping color in my early Pheasant Hill drawings at the Vermont house dining table; Brittany, Julie, and Patti at Huntsman; Jim Ingebritsen; Stanislas Boivin-Champeaux; Museum art printer extraordinaire, MP at Atelier; Mark Mendelsohn; for doing an amazing job with my acrylic art prints, Scott and Charlene Mangelson; Francesco Bottigliero at Brunello Cucinelli HQ in Solomeo; John Howard; select sponsors who were so great, Campagnolo, Adidas, Vans, Vuarnet, Revo, Fischer Skis, Flying Tigers, DuPont, Orvis, Tibor, Dynamic Skis, Rossignol, and Cannondale; Roger Allenbaugh for WindTunnel; in-law, friend and wonderful reviewer of my book draft, Julia Halberstam; Grove Mower for book advice and a solid read; Gavin Pierce, Daniel, Franz, and Cory at Porsche SLC; photographer, artist, and friend, Michael Furman; former *Fortune* magazine managing editor, guitar rocker, friend, and amazing edit advisor for this book, Eric Pooley; my WindTunnel support team: Alpine Olympic and World Cup superstar Ted Ligety, fashion maven Marion Zaniello, Clare Ashforth, Mike Pell, Courtney Harkins of the US Ski Team, Doug Augustine, Jake Wolf, and Tom Kelly (who also helped shepherd our work with USSA so long ago); book advisor, Sharon Woodhouse; exceptional editor and detail master, Jesse Winter; layout star, Victoria Wolf; and from the Wayback Machine, Fenno and Barwick—"Stairway"!

Forgive me for any omissions. Those of you who have been part of my life know who you are and know this: you are important to me, more important than these words can indicate.

ABOUT THE AUTHOR

DAVID WIENER is an internationally recognized designer and artist. He developed his sense of design and art at an early age, leading him to create custom Porsches and BMWs, along with a wide variety of iconic products, vehicles, logos and brands for such global names as Ferrari, Porsche, the US Ski Team, Columbia PFG, Ben & Jerry's, Ganassi Racing, and many others.

David lives in Park City, Utah with his wife, Kate, where they raised their three sons, Weston, Hans and Enzo. When not working, David is active in all things that inspire his work: skiing, saltwater fly-fishing, playing guitar, bird hunting, driving on the track and mountain biking. Some of his best ideas have been inspired by time spent laughing, mixing drinks, and cooking meals with clients, family, and friends.